The Greek
SLOW COOKER

The *Greek*
SLOW COOKER

Easy, Delicious Recipes From
the Heart of the Mediterranean

ELENI VONISSAKOU
Creator of The Foodie Corner

PAGE STREET
PUBLISHING CO.

PAGE STREET
PUBLISHING CO.

Copyright © 2019 Eleni Vonissakou

First published in 2019 by
Page Street Publishing Co.
27 Congress Street, Suite 105
Salem, MA 01970
www.pagestreetpublishing.com

Distributed by Macmillan, sales in Canada by The Canadian Manda Group.

23 22 21 20 19   1 2 3 4 5

ISBN-13: 978-1-62414-748-7
ISBN-10: 1-62414-748-8

Library of Congress Control Number: 2018964664

Cover and book design by Laura Gallant for Page Street Publishing Co.
Photography by Eleni Vonissakou
Cover photography by Eleni Vonissakou and Constantina Papageorgiou
Author photograph by Danai Issaris

Printed and bound in China

In loving memory
of my aunties,
JOSIE AND ANGIE

Contents

THE BEGINNING. MY SLOW COOKER AND I.

I love slow cookers. I adore them. They are the best invention since the wheel. Oh, okay . . . maybe there were a couple other good ones in between. But if you are reading this book, chances are you love your slow cooker too. If you don't, well, I hope you fall for it while trying some of my recipes!

Before I tell my favorite story about how I got to know this wonderful appliance, let me introduce myself. My name is Eleni and I am half Greek (Dad) and half English (Mum). Although I was born in England, I was raised in Athens, Greece. The only time I've spent in the UK, apart from holidays, were my student days. That is also when I started to cook, right about when my fondness for baked beans on toast started to wear thin, sometime in year three. Fast forward a few years (okay, more than a few) and I'm enjoying cooking so much that I'm a food blogger.

So how did my love affair with slow cookers begin? Well, my brother, who lives in England, bought himself one a while back. I had already heard of these appliances but didn't know many details about them. During a visit, he prepared a delicious slow-cooked stew for my mum and I. Since slow cookers didn't even exist in Greece, I never considered getting one at the time. However, on my mum's next visit, she went out and bought one, carried it in her hand luggage all the way from England to Greece and delivered it to my house, saying "You have to have one!" She was so right, as mums usually are.

But was it love at first cook? Hm. If I'm being completely honest, I was a little disappointed to begin with. At the time, I mostly cooked from recipes and could not for the life of me find any good ones for the slow cooker. They all seemed a bit strange to me, consisting mainly of meat, a tin of store-bought cream-of-whatever soup and a packet of seasoning mix. I've nothing against these kitchen cupboard staples, and I might have tried them had I been able to find them easily in Greece. But I think I would have eventually started craving something with a fresher feel to it, especially if I would be using the slow cooker often. I'd nearly given up, when I came across a fantastic blog with lots and lots of slow cooker recipes. They weren't all from scratch, but there were enough to get me going. And most had ingredients that could easily be substituted with ones available in my country. That was it. I was hooked.

I mean, what's not to love? So easy to use even an inexperienced cook can produce gorgeous food, and so undemanding of our attention that we can get on with our busy lives while the slow cooker makes sure we have a delicious dinner at the end of the day. There is also another huge advantage. Coming from a country with hot summers, I can tell you that during those months when I feel I might melt if I put the oven on, my slow cookers come to the rescue. Why? Because they don't heat up the kitchen! I have never understood those who say this appliance is only for winter. If there is any time you surely want to be using it, it's during a heat wave! Unless, of course, you can get by on just salad. I can't. Next time the temperature soars, try cooking in the slow cooker and you'll know what I mean.

After jumping on the slow cooker bandwagon, I gradually became more confident adapting conventional recipes, until I was creating my own. My best "high-fiving myself" moments were when I successfully adapted Greek classics and got delicious results. After only a few of these successes, the seed for a book was planted in my mind. Fast-forward a few more years (and a food blog and a business importing slow cookers to Greece), and here we are.

Greek food is very well suited to the slow cooker. There will always be things that just don't work in it, like pastry for example. Fried foods also can't really be replicated. But anything made in a saucepan and most things made in the oven can be adapted with fabulous results. In fact, you might be surprised by what you can create! Go on, take another peek at the table of contents!

I am so excited to bring real Greek food to your slow cooker. My recipes are for dishes that one could expect to find on a family dinner table in Greece today. Some classic, some traditional, some with a small twist. All beloved by Greek people. I really hope you enjoy them.

Kali orexi! (Enjoy your meal!)

Eleni

BEFORE WE START . . .

I have several slow cooker cookbooks on my shelf. They all seem to start off talking in detail about appliance models and brands. I am going to proceed on the assumption that you already have a slow cooker, so I will spare you the long paragraphs about which to choose.

Having said that, I do need to mention a couple things I consider very important about the different types of cookers and the way we use them. I will be as quick as I can; I know this is the boring bit. But it will help down the line.

Sequence of ingredients as they are added to the slow cooker

Slow cookers have a reputation of being great for just "plopping everything in" and letting it cook away. This does work in many cases, but for some recipes the order in which the ingredients are layered makes quite a difference. This is especially true when cooking without much liquid. Make sure to follow the instructions as stated in order to get the best result.

Ceramic inserts versus metal (aluminum, stove-top safe) inserts

There is supposed to be no difference between the two types of inserts, but in my experience the metal pots cook a little faster and a bit more evenly. This was confirmed by one of the UK brands I work with; apparently, the aluminum they are made of distributes heat better. This might differ from brand to brand, so it's not set in stone; it's just something to have in mind. In a few recipes, I have made a distinction in cooking time between the two types of insert. Keep an eye on the food and use your common sense to decide how to proceed in each case.

Slow cooker capacity and cooking time

Cooking time, when comparing equal amounts of food, depends on the capacity of the insert. To keep it simple, the more empty space there is in the pot, the faster the food will cook (so less food = less time / more food = more time). One 3-pound (1.4-kg) chicken will cook much faster in a 6-quart (5.7-L) cooker than it will in a 3-quart (2.8-L) cooker.

The recipes in this book were all created and tested in 7-quart (6.5-L) cookers, but there would be no significant difference if the recipes are made in a 6-quart (5.7-L) cooker instead.

Servings

The number of servings for most recipes is four to six. Four portions in a 7-quart (6.5-L) cooker may seem too few, but here in Greece people tend to prefer the larger cookers. For this reason, some of the cooking times are shorter than one would expect. This is due to the amount of ingredients in relation to the cooker size. If you are using a different size or want to add more ingredients, take note of all the above information and adapt accordingly. In some cases, however, it might not be a good idea to increase quantities (namely the cakes, pies, omelets and bread) as the edges might start to overcook before the center is cooked through.

Cooking times vary

Always have this in mind when working with a slow cooker. The slightest thing can make a difference. The appliance capacity, the insert type, the brand, the model within the brand, the ingredients, the temperature of the ingredients . . . you get the picture. The good thing is that it's actually hard to ruin food in the slow cooker, so being precise with times is only important when you want the absolute maximum perfection for your dish. A few "trial and error" attempts won't leave you hungry, and the food will still be yummy. Unfortunately, there is no way for anyone to tell you exactly how long your cooker needs for a particular recipe, so when trying something new, my best advice is to keep an eye on it toward the end.

A few last words about Greek food and ingredients

The recipes in this book are for classic dishes cooked over and over throughout Greece. In order to get the closest possible result, I strongly urge you to find the best, most authentic raw materials you can. Greek cooking doesn't have a myriad of ingredients; they are usually few, but good quality. It's worth the investment.

- Try to avoid substituting items. Things like tomatoes and rice make a difference depending on their specific type and preparation. For example, fresh tomato won't behave like canned or jarred, and arborio rice will give a different result to long grain.

- In certain recipes, you will come across some typically Greek ingredients which may not be available at regular supermarkets. Check your area for any Greek delis and Mediterranean or Middle Eastern markets, or search online for Greek and Mediterranean products. In some cases, I've offered alternative suggestions for some of the harder-to-find products, but the original ingredient will always offer the best results for the dish, so it's well worth the effort to track it down.

- Some of the measurements for dry ingredients in this book are volume-based (cups) for ease of reference. Being European, I always prefer to weigh my ingredients in order to be sure I have exact quantities. I highly recommend you invest in a small set of weighing scales (there are some very economical ones on the market) as these will help you achieve perfect results with your cooking every time.

- Unless otherwise stated in the ingredient list, the weight mentioned for vegetables is the weight after preparation. We all have different ways we peel potatoes, for example, so I feel this is the most accurate.

- Greek food is rarely served piping hot. It is enjoyed warm, sometimes even at room temperature. This is another reason Greek cuisine is well suited to the slow cooker, as food cooked this way always benefits from a rest before serving.

Let's get to those recipes!

Making a sling for easy removal of cakes and pies

1.
Cut two 25-inch (63-cm) pieces of aluminum foil.

2.
Fold each piece of foil lengthwise three times.

3.

4.

5.
Leaving the foil underneath, line the pot with a long piece of parchment paper.

6.
Tuck the ends of the foil inwards, overlapping the parchment paper.

7.
After adding the mixture, lay a paper towel on top.

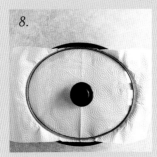
8.
Secure tautly with the lid.

NO-FUSS, SUCCULENT POULTRY *and* GAME

IN GREECE, THE MOST POPULAR MEAT in this category is undoubtedly chicken and rooster. Rabbit, although not as common as it once was, is still frequently enjoyed, especially on the island of Crete. The recipes in this chapter are based on these three types of white meat.

Chicken, probably the most versatile of all meat, is widely consumed throughout Greece. For city folk, a chicken or rooster "from the village"—often a valuable gift from a relative in a more rural area—is always good news. The slow cooker is without question the best way to cook even the toughest organic chicken to juicy perfection.

If you're wondering which part of the chicken or rooster is best for slow cooking, my vote goes to the leg (thighs and drumsticks). I've noticed that in some countries people tend to prefer the breast, but extended cooking can sometimes dry that out, especially when it's filleted. Thighs and drumsticks stay deliciously soft and succulent. Whole chicken is also a great idea for the slow cooker. One helpful tip is to put the bird in the slow cooker breast down so it sits at least partly in the juices produced during cooking. Leave the skin on until after it's cooked, then discard.

Rabbit is trickier to cook regardless of method, since it is a leaner meat. However, once you get to know exactly how long it needs in your own slow cooker, the result will be beautifully tender. Personally, I don't find any notable difference between the various parts of a rabbit, so any cut is fine for slow cooking.

If you're a fan of white meat, these delicious classic Greek dishes could well find their way into your weekly meal plan.

Hearty Egg-Lemon Chicken Soup

(KOTOSOUPA AVGOLEMONO)

Who doesn't love a bowl of hot chicken soup? Almost every country has its own traditions for this meal, and Greek chicken soup is one of the most famous out there. This is probably due to the *avgolemono*, the egg-lemon, which does indeed make it rather special and different from its "cousins" elsewhere. Traditional *Kotosoupa Avgolemono* doesn't have vegetables (it's just chicken, water, rice and egg-lemon), although nowadays most people (including me!) do add some for extra flavor and goodness. The vegetables in this recipe are a flavorful addition to an already tasty traditional soup.

2 lb (900 g) boneless, skinless chicken thigh fillets, cut into large pieces

1 whole onion

2 cups (250 g) potatoes, cut into 1-inch (2.5-cm) cubes

2/3 cup (85 g) carrot, sliced to 1/4-inch (6-mm) thickness

1/2 cup (60 g) celery, sliced to 1/4-inch (6-mm) thickness

6 cups (1.4 L) hot chicken stock

2 tbsp (30 ml) olive oil

1 tsp salt

1/2 tsp black pepper

1/3 cup (60 g) arborio rice

2 eggs

1/4 cup (60 ml) lemon juice, plus extra, to serve

Freshly ground black pepper, to taste

Fresh crusty bread

In the slow cooker insert, combine the chicken thighs, onion, potatoes, carrot, celery, chicken stock, olive oil, salt and pepper.

Cook on low for 7 to 8 hours, or until the vegetables are soft and the chicken is cooked through. Remove the onion.

Add the rice and continue cooking for another 20 to 40 minutes, until the rice is very soft.

In a large bowl, beat the eggs while slowly adding the lemon juice. Turn the slow cooker off and bring the bowl next to it. Slowly start spooning hot soup from the insert into the bowl. Start with a tablespoon (15 ml) at a time, gradually increasing the quantity (a 1/4- or 1/2-cup [60- or 120-ml] measuring cup is good for this). Whisk the mixture continuously while adding the hot liquid, to avoid scrambling the eggs. When about 3 cups (720 ml) of the soup has been transferred (tilt your slow cooker to help, if necessary) and the bowl is hot to the touch, pour the egg-lemon mixture back into the insert. Using the side handles, move the slow cooker in a circular motion so everything is distributed evenly.

Serve immediately with lots of extra lemon juice, freshly ground pepper and good crusty bread.

Rooster in Red Sauce with Hilopites

(KOKORAS ME HILOPITES)

A rather special dish, *Kokoras me Hilopites* is one that elicits oohs and ahhs even upon the mere mention of the name. "Sunday food" at its best, the rooster is prepared in a tomato sauce and served with either traditional Greek short pasta (*hilopites*) or a thick spaghetti such as bucatini.

Cooking a rooster isn't as easy as cooking a conventional chicken from the supermarket. It's tougher and it can be hard to keep it juicy and succulent. Unless, of course, you use a slow cooker, which is by far the best way to cook this demanding meat.

¾ cup (110 g) finely chopped onion, lightly packed

3 lb (1.4 kg) free-range rooster, bone in and skin on, cut into large portions

1 (14.5-oz [411-g]) can diced tomatoes, no salt added, with liquid

1 cup (240 ml) tomato passata (see Note)

3 tbsp (45 ml) olive oil

1¼ tsp (7 g) salt, divided

2 tsp (4 g) sweet paprika

1 tsp thyme

1 tsp sugar

½ tsp freshly ground black pepper

½ tsp dried oregano

½ tsp dried basil

3–3½ cups (780–900 ml) boiling water

12 oz (340 g) square hilopites

Kefalotyri, mizithra or crumbled feta cheese, to serve

Spread the onion across the bottom of the slow cooker insert. Place the rooster pieces on top of the onion and pour in the tomatoes, passata and oil. Add 1 teaspoon of salt, the paprika, thyme, sugar, pepper, oregano and basil. Cook on low for 6 to 7 hours, or until the rooster meat is falling off the bone.

Without turning off the slow cooker, carefully remove the rooster with a slotted spoon and transfer it to a plate to cool enough for handling. Make sure to check for any stray bones in the tomato sauce.

Next, measure the liquid from the slow cooker. The easiest way is to tip the appliance to the side by lifting one of the side handles, then ladle the sauce into a measuring cup. There should be about 3 to 3½ cups (720 to 900 ml) of sauce. (It's fine if a few tablespoons stay in the bottom of the insert.) Return the sauce to the slow cooker and add enough boiling water to bring the total amount of liquid up to 6 cups (1.4 L). Turn the cooker to high, add the remaining ¼ teaspoon of salt and let everything warm up again for 5 to 10 minutes.

Add the hilopites to the slow cooker and stir well. Cook for 30 to 40 minutes, stirring well every 10 to 15 minutes, or more often if needed toward the end of the cook time. After 30 minutes, try them often to avoid overcooking them. If the pasta absorbs all the liquid and still hasn't cooked, add hot water ¼ cup (60 ml) at a time. The result should be almost as "soupy" as risotto, because the pasta will continue to absorb sauce and thicken after cooking. If the pasta is starting to overcook, add ¼ cup (60 ml) of cold water to halt the cooking process.

While the hilopites are cooking, pick the cooled rooster meat off the bones, leaving as many large pieces as you can; the meat will be so soft it will shred easily. Add it to the slow cooker 5 minutes before the end to warm through.

Serve immediately, with lots of grated kefalotyri, mizithra or crumbled feta cheese.

Note: Tomato passata is a medium-thick juice made of crushed and strained tomatoes. You can find it—and square hilopites—online or in Greek markets. You can use tomato puree in place of tomato passata and orzo in place of square hilopites if needed.

White Wine Chicken with Orzo

(KOTOPOULO YIOUVETSI LEFKO)

Are you familiar with the term *yiouvetsi*? If you are, you probably have in mind a dish with meat and orzo in tomato, something like my Tomato-Braised Beef with Orzo (Yiouvetsi Moshari) on page 33. In Greece, we also have the so-called "white yiouvetsi" dishes—white meaning without tomato. The ingredients are simple, but create a wonderful, delicately flavorful result.

This was one of the first recipes I tried, back when the book was just a little idea in a corner of my mind. I was so pleased with how it turned out that I immediately jotted down the recipe. Cooking the orzo pasta in the slow cooker at the end needs a little attention the first couple times, but once you get the hang of it the recipe is easy. A perfect midweek meal.

1 cup (140 g) finely chopped onion, lightly packed

2 lb (900 g) boneless, skinless chicken thigh fillets

½ cup (120 ml) good-quality white wine

¼ cup (60 ml) freshly squeezed lemon juice

2 tbsp (30 ml) olive oil

¼ cup (15 g) fresh parsley, finely chopped, tightly packed

1 tsp salt

¾ tsp black pepper

1 tsp dried thyme

8½ oz (240 g) orzo pasta

1 cup (240 ml) boiling water, plus extra if needed

Grated Greek Gruyère or kefalotyri cheese, to serve

In the slow cooker insert, combine the onion, chicken, wine, lemon juice, olive oil, parsley, salt, pepper and thyme.

Cook on low for 5 to 6 hours, or until the chicken is tender and falling apart.

Turn the cooker to high and add the orzo. Stir and cook on high until the orzo has absorbed most of the liquid already in the slow cooker. Start adding hot water, ½ cup (120 ml) to begin with and then ¼ cup (60 ml) at a time, as needed for the pasta to cook through. Total cooking time for the pasta should be 25 to 35 minutes. Turn the slow cooker off when the orzo is al dente and the consistency is quite wet and "sloppy" looking, since the pasta will continue to absorb liquid as it rests.

Serve immediately with the grated cheese.

Oven-Style Lemon Chicken and Potatoes

(KOTOPOULO ME PATATES)

A classic of classics. There are a couple names for this dish: "chicken and potatoes," or "chicken in the oven"—somewhat plain names for food that is anything but. I don't think there is a Greek household anywhere in which this dish isn't made at least a couple times a month. If there is, I'm sure it's sorely missed.

Main players here are the chicken, potatoes, lemon, oregano and lots of olive oil. Variations are numerous but the result is always delicious, and making it in the slow cooker means beautifully tender meat and very tasty potatoes. The process might seem a little fussy, but it's worth taking the extra steps to ensure the flavors are well dispersed.

2½ lb (1.1 kg) peeled potatoes, cut into medium-sized pieces

3 tbsp (45 ml) olive oil, divided

1½ tsp (9 g) salt, divided

1 tbsp (15 ml) whole-grain mustard, plus extra, to serve

2 tsp (10 g) mild garlic paste

2 tsp (4 g) dried oregano

2 tsp (4 g) dried thyme

2 tsp (4 g) sweet paprika

1 tsp lemon zest

¾ tsp freshly ground black pepper

5 tbsp (75 ml) freshly squeezed lemon juice, divided

4 (11–12 oz [310–340 g]) whole chicken legs, bone in, skin on

2 medium onions, halved

Greek salad, optional

Place the potatoes in the bottom of the slow cooker insert, drizzle with 1 tablespoon (15 ml) of the olive oil and sprinkle with ½ teaspoon of the salt.

In a small bowl, combine the mustard, garlic paste, oregano, thyme, paprika, lemon zest, pepper and the remaining teaspoon of salt. Add the remaining 2 tablespoons (30 ml) of olive oil and mix with a fork to incorporate.

Fill a tablespoon with this mixture and combine it with 3 tablespoons (45 ml) of the lemon juice. Pour over the potatoes.

Rub the rest of the thick mixture all over the chicken legs, getting under the skin wherever possible without removing it.

Place the chicken on top of the potatoes, skin side up. Then put the onions on top of the chicken, cut side down, and pour the remaining 2 tablespoons (30 ml) of lemon juice into the slow cooker.

Cook on low for 7 to 8 hours, or until the potatoes are easily pierced with a knife and the chicken is falling off the bone. Remove the lid from the slow cooker and let stand for 5 to 10 minutes, then carefully remove the chicken with a wide slotted spoon. Remove and discard the skins and arrange the chicken pieces on a platter. Garnish with the potatoes and spoon some of the juices on top, or transfer some into a small jug or gravy boat and serve on the side.

Enjoy with some extra mustard and a Greek salad.

Rabbit and Shallot Stew

(KOUNELI STIFADO)

Stifado is probably the most famous rabbit dish in Greece. It's a classic, and although recipes can differ, and some even use other types of meat, certain ingredients are always included. The main one is shallots, the signature ingredient of all stifados.

The actual dish is said to have been brought to Greece in the thirteenth century by the Venetians. Some maintain that the word stifado comes from the Italian *stufato*, which means stew; others claim that it comes from the word *stufa,* which means oven.

Whatever the origin, stifado is a rich, wintry dish full of intense flavors and very well suited to the slow cooker.

---

3 tbsp (45 ml) olive oil, divided

3 tbsp (45 g) butter, divided

3 lb (1.4 kg) rabbit, bone in, cut into portions

1½ lb (680 g) shallots, peeled and left whole (see Note)

½ cup (120 ml) Merlot or other red wine

½ cup (120 ml) hot chicken stock

1 tbsp (15 ml) balsamic vinegar

1 tbsp (15 ml) tomato paste

1 tbsp (15 ml) honey

1 tsp salt

½ tsp allspice

½ tsp cinnamon

¼ tsp black pepper

1 tsp dried rosemary

1 tbsp (8 g) cornstarch

1 tbsp (15 ml) cold water

Rice, French fries, bread or salad, to serve

Add 2 tablespoons (30 ml) of the olive oil and 2 tablespoons (30 g) of the butter to a large nonstick frying pan and heat over medium-high. Sauté the rabbit for 6 to 8 minutes, or until it takes on a nice golden-brown color. Transfer it to the slow cooker using tongs.

Turn the heat to medium-low, add 1 tablespoon (15 ml) of the olive oil, 1 tablespoon (15 g) of the butter and the shallots. Cook gently for 15 minutes, or until nicely browned on all sides. Transfer to the slow cooker.

Pour the wine, chicken stock, balsamic vinegar, tomato paste, honey, salt, allspice, cinnamon and pepper into the warm frying pan. It won't bubble very much but that is okay. Stir for about 30 seconds, or until the paste and honey have melted, and tip everything into the slow cooker. Sprinkle the rosemary over the top.

Cook on low for 5½ to 6½ hours, or until the meat is falling off the bone and the shallots are very soft.

When the rabbit is ready, tilt the slow cooker to the side and ladle some of the liquid into a measuring cup. Take as much as you want to make the sauce (at least 1 cup [240 ml]). In a separate small bowl, measure out 1 tablespoon (8 g) of cornstarch per cup of cooking liquid and add an equal amount of cold water (1 tablespoon [15 ml]). Stir the cornstarch mixture until you get a smooth white slurry. Add this slurry to the warm cooking liquid, stir and microwave for 1½ to 2 minutes to thicken slightly.

Serve the rabbit and sauce with rice or French fries or just some good crusty bread and a nice salad.

Note: The shallots in stifado should remain whole. Here's a useful tip passed on from my Greek grandmother to my mum when she was teaching her to cook Greek dishes: To ensure the shallots don't fall apart during cooking, make sure you don't cut the whole base off while peeling. Using a sharp knife, "shave" the base to remove the roots but don't cut too deep.

Greek Easter Soup, My Mum's Way

(MAGIRITSA)

Magiritsa. Pronounced "mageereetsa." To me, it's synonymous with church hymns, red eggs, lit candles, late-night feasting and loud fireworks, as it's the soup we have after midnight mass on Holy Saturday. After the forty days of Lent, during which those who observe haven't eaten any meat, fish or dairy, it's important to prepare the stomach for the rich meal of Easter Sunday. Magiritsa is supposed to do just that. Traditionally it's made with lamb offal, which is a good way to ensure no part of the lamb destined to be cooked on the spit on Easter Sunday is wasted.

At my house, we never went for the offal version. My mum preferred to use chicken liver, which is much lighter in taste. Since I absolutely hate liver of any kind, this was the only time she made me eat it, insisting it was "good for me." I loved the soup itself, so as long as the pieces were cut small, I could live with that. Nowadays I still dislike liver, but Easter isn't the same without this Magiritsa. Its spring freshness, silky texture and citrusy tang make it a delicious soup, which can easily be enjoyed at any time of year.

3 tbsp (45 ml) olive oil, divided

3 tbsp (45 g) butter, divided

¾ cup (110 g) finely chopped onion, lightly packed

3 cups (310 g) finely chopped spring onions, green parts included, lightly packed

18 oz (510 g) chicken liver

12 oz (340 g) chopped Romaine lettuce

1⅓ cups / 3½ oz (100 g) fresh dill, cut into ½-inch (2.5-cm) pieces, stalks included, very tightly packed

¼ cup (60 ml) brandy

1 tsp salt

1 tsp lemon pepper

6 cups (1.4 L) hot chicken stock

¼ cup (40 g) arborio rice

2 eggs

¼ cup (60 ml) lemon juice, plus extra, to serve

Freshly ground black pepper

Hard boiled eggs, optional

Crusty bread, optional

Heat 1 tablespoon (15 ml) of the olive oil and 1 tablespoon (15 g) of the butter in a large nonstick frying pan over medium heat. Add the onion and let it cook gently for 3 to 4 minutes. Add the spring onions, stir well and let them cook for 10 minutes, until soft and wilted, stirring often (turn the heat down if the mixture starts burning). Transfer the contents of the pan to the slow cooker insert.

Return the pan to the heat, add 1 more tablespoon (15 ml) of the olive oil with 1 tablespoon (15 g) of the butter and turn the heat back up to medium. Add the chicken liver and cook gently for about 7 minutes, or until the juices that are released evaporate and the meat is sizzling.

While the chicken liver is cooking, add the lettuce and dill to the slow cooker on top of the onions.

Pour the brandy onto the liver in the pan and let it bubble, still on medium heat, for a few seconds. Tip everything, including the juices, into the slow cooker over the greens.

Add the remaining olive oil and butter, salt and lemon pepper to the slow cooker. Pour the hot stock over everything and let the soup cook on low for 7 to 8 hours.

Stir in the rice and let the soup cook until it softens, another 30 to 45 minutes.

When ready, beat the eggs in a medium-sized bowl while slowly adding the lemon juice. Turn the slow cooker off and bring the bowl next to it. Slowly transfer small quantities of hot soup to the egg-lemon mixture while beating continuously. Use a measuring cup (the best size is ¼ cup [60 ml] or ½ cup [120 ml]), starting with small quantities, about 1 tablespoon (15 ml)-worth, and gradually increasing the amount. The more hot liquid transferred to the eggs, the better. When the bowl is quite full and the mixture is hot, pour it all back into the slow cooker with the rest of the soup. Using the handles, move the slow cooker around so the egg-lemon sauce becomes incorporated. Cover with the lid until it's time to serve the soup.

Serve with extra lemon juice if desired, freshly ground black pepper, hard-boiled eggs and lots of crusty bread.

Oregano-Seasoned Rabbit

(KOUNELI RIGANATO)

Oregano is possibly the most popular dry herb in Greece, growing easily and freely high up on mountains, on rocky islands or even in city suburbs. It is very often used in cooking and there are many dishes called *riganato,* in which oregano is the main herb. It is frequently combined with lemon or white wine and mustard to give a delicious tasting sauce to the meat it is cooked with.

My version of riganato also has a bit of saffron. It may be a lesser known fact, but Greece produces a very high quality red saffron, known here as *Krokos Kozanis*, which is highly sought after and exported to many countries. Interestingly, saffron doesn't feature much in Greek cooking, so you wouldn't normally come across it in a dish like this. I think it makes an interesting addition.

---

2 tbsp (30 ml) olive oil

2 tbsp (30 g) butter

3 lb (1.4 kg) rabbit, bone in, cut into portions

2 medium onions, halved

3 tbsp (45 ml) freshly squeezed lemon juice

1 tbsp (15 g) dried oregano

2 tsp (10 g) mild garlic paste

1 tsp prepared yellow mustard

1 tsp salt

½ tsp lemon pepper

5 threads of saffron

½ cup (120 ml) hot chicken stock

1 (8-oz [225-g]) package long-grain parboiled rice (I use a parboiled and wild rice mix)

Heat the olive oil and butter in a large nonstick frying pan over medium-high heat and brown the rabbit on all sides, about 6 to 8 minutes. Transfer it to the slow cooker insert along with any juices from the pan. Place the onion halves on top of the meat, cut side down.

Stir the lemon juice, oregano, garlic paste, mustard, salt, lemon pepper and saffron threads into the hot chicken stock. Pour the mixture over the rabbit, cover and cook on low for 5½ to 6½ hours, or until the meat is falling off the bone.

In a saucepan, ladle out 1 cup (240 ml) of the cooking liquid, then add as much water as needed to get the total amount of liquid required on package instructions to cook the rice. Bring it to a boil, then add the rice and cook according to the instructions, for about 15 to 30 minutes.

Serve the rabbit with the rice and use the remaining juice from the slow cooker as a sauce.

Succulent Chicken and Okra Stew

(KOTOPOULO ME BAMIES)

If there was ever a "love it or hate it" dish in Greece, it's this one. The chicken is loved by most. The okra, on the other hand . . . not so much! Some people hate it with a passion. I think this has much to do with the "gel" that these curious little vegetables can exude during cooking. If buying fresh okra, which is actually quite small here in Greece, you are supposed to follow a whole procedure to make sure this gel disappears. It involves vinegar and laying the okra out to dry in the sun. Not very convenient to the modern lifestyle, especially if you live somewhere that isn't so sunny. Frozen okra makes it possible to enjoy this very interesting dish without all the hassle. It's been prepped beforehand, so any gel-like texture is kept to a minimum.

Okra is quite delicate and since it doesn't need as long as chicken to cook, it should be added halfway through so it doesn't get mushy. Make sure it's fully defrosted when it's added, otherwise it will interrupt the cooking process and make the sauce too runny.

¾ cup (110 g) finely chopped onion, lightly packed

2 lb (900 g) boneless, skinless chicken thigh fillets

1 cup (240 ml) tomato passata (see Note)

2 tbsp (30 ml) balsamic vinegar

1 tbsp (15 ml) honey

1 tsp sweet paprika

1 tsp salt, divided

¼ tsp black pepper

2 tbsp (30 ml) olive oil

1 (2-lb [900-g]) package frozen okra, fully thawed, brought to room temperature

Feta cheese, to serve

Fresh crusty bread, to serve

In the slow cooker insert, combine the onion, chicken thighs, passata, balsamic vinegar, honey, paprika, ½ teaspoon of salt, the black pepper and olive oil. Cook on low for about 2 hours if your cooker has an aluminum pot or 3 hours if the pot is ceramic.

Add the thawed okra and the rest of the salt, and cook on low for an additional 2 hours for the aluminum pot or 3 hours for the ceramic pot. The chicken should be fall-apart tender and the okra should be soft. Some of the okra may be breaking down, but it shouldn't be completely mushy.

Serve with feta cheese and crusty bread.

Note: Tomato passata is a medium-thick juice made of crushed and strained raw tomatoes. You should be able to find it in local stores or Greek markets, or online. You could also use a tomato puree in place of the passata, though results may vary due to some differences in water content and volume.

DELICIOUS,
FALL–APART TENDER
MEAT

ARE YOU ONE OF THOSE PEOPLE who sees a plate of vegetables and says "Okay . . . so, what's for dinner?" It's a question many Greeks would ask when presented with anything other than a huge portion of meat. So of course, Greek cuisine has lots of delicious dishes featuring mainly pork, lamb, goat and beef.

Interestingly, it was pork that was originally served here on Christmas Day. Turkey made its appearance in recent decades as Christmas became more Westernized, but many families do still prefer pork for their festivities. Lamb or goat are also very popular choices for special occasions and parties. Beef, now a major part of people's diets, is in fact the least traditional as it was more difficult to farm cows in Greece due to terrain and climate.

It is important to keep a few things in mind when talking about meat in relation to slow cookers. Basically, not all cuts are suitable. This is especially true with beef and pork. One of the main problems I encountered while getting to know my slow cooker was achieving the beautifully tender meat described in American or English recipes.

I have since learned that there were a number of possible reasons for this. For one, meat is cut differently from country to country. So, some cuts you read about might not even exist in your country. Also, even if you find the exact same piece, the animal was raised differently and probably slaughtered at a different age. The meat itself may then have been aged for a different amount of time. All these factors have a huge impact on a recipe.

For Greek meats, I have come to the following conclusion. When cooking beef, the best cuts are those with collagen (e.g., shank with or without bone and certain parts of the chuck) and when cooking pork, the best are neck and knuckle. Lamb and goat work better in the slow cooker overall, so any cut suitable for stewing or braising is a good choice.

I suggest that for the recipes in this chapter you choose tried and tested cuts of meat that you know you love making in the slow cooker. If you're not sure, ask your butcher for suggestions.

Tomato-Braised Beef with Orzo

(YIOUVETSI MOSHARI)

This *yiouvetsi* is up there with rooster in red sauce in terms of how special it is. Another dish fit for the Sunday family dinner table, yiouvetsi is a favorite of many Greek people. The original version featured lamb or goat, then came the beef and chicken variations, and in recent years some interesting seafood or mushroom yiouvetsi dishes have appeared too. The most popular seems to be the beef version.

The word yiouvetsi actually refers to the clay vessel originally used for this dish, which in conventional cooking is started on the stovetop then baked in the oven. My version also starts on the stovetop but finishes off— where else?—in the slow cooker.

5 tbsp (75 ml) olive oil, divided

¾ cup (110 g) finely chopped onion, lightly packed

⅔ cup (85 g) coarsely grated carrot

⅓ cup (40 g) finely chopped celery, without leaves, lightly packed

1 tbsp (15 ml) tomato paste

2½ lb (1.1 kg) beef, in large chunks (boneless or crosscut shank works well, or use your favorite cut for the slow cooker)

½ cup (120 ml) good quality red wine such as Merlot

1 (14-oz [411-g]) can diced tomatoes, no salt added, with liquid

1 tsp garlic paste

1 tsp sugar

1 tsp salt

¼ tsp black pepper

1 bay leaf

3 cups (720 ml) boiling water, plus more if needed

11 oz (310 g) orzo pasta

Kefalotyri, mizithra or feta cheese, to serve

In a large frying pan, heat 1 tablespoon (15 ml) of the olive oil over medium heat and gently cook the onion until it turns translucent and starts to soften, for about 2 to 3 minutes, depending on the size of your pan.

Add the carrot and celery and continue to cook until they are soft, about 8 minutes, stirring frequently. Add the tomato paste, stir well and let it cook for 1 to 2 minutes. Transfer the mixture to the slow cooker. Wipe the pan with some paper towels if necessary.

Return the pan to the stove and turn the heat to medium-high. Add 2 tablespoons (30 ml) of the olive oil and the meat. Brown the meat on all sides for about 10 minutes, working in batches if necessary so the meat isn't crowded in the pan. Place the browned beef on top of the sautéed vegetables.

Pour the wine into the hot frying pan and let it bubble for a few seconds, while stirring with a wooden spoon to get any browned bits up. Tip the contents of the pan into the slow cooker and turn off the stove.

In the still-hot pan, mix the tomatoes with the last 2 tablespoons (30 ml) of olive oil, the garlic paste, sugar, salt and pepper. Pour onto the meat. Add the bay leaf and cook on low for 6 to 8 hours, or until the meat is fall-apart tender.

When the meat is ready, boil the 3 cups (720 ml) of water. Remove and discard the bay leaf. Turn the slow cooker to high, add the water and orzo and stir well. Continue cooking on high for 30 to 40 minutes, or until the orzo is fully cooked and has absorbed most of the sauce. Ideally, the consistency should be that of risotto (quite wet), since the pasta will continue to cook and thicken after the slow cooker is turned off. If the pasta is still grainy in the center but there is no liquid in the pot, add some boiling water ¼ cup (60 ml) at a time. If the pasta is soft and in danger of overcooking, turn off the cooker and add 2 tablespoons (30 ml) of cold water to halt the cooking process.

Serve immediately with a generous sprinkling of grated kefalotyri, mizithra or some crumbled feta.

Beef and Quince in Sweet and Sour Gravy

(SOFIGADO)

SERVES 4—6

This version of *sofigado* originates from the Ionian island of Lefkada, in western Greece. It is said that the dish dates to Venetian times, when the islands of the Ionian Sea were under occupation by the Venetian Empire. Judging by the name this makes sense, as it sounds like a word with a Latin root rather than a Greek one. The interesting thing is that beef and quince stew is actually a Middle Eastern classic. The spices are different, but the main ingredients are the same. It just goes to show how intertwined the history of world cuisines is.

Sofigado has a gorgeous sweet and sour flavor due to the use of vinegar and *petimezi*, or grape must syrup. The gravy that's created during the slow cooking process is truly wonderful.

---

4 tbsp (60 ml) olive oil, divided

2 lb (900 g) beef (shank works well)

1 cup (140 g) finely chopped onion, lightly packed

¼ cup (60 ml) red wine vinegar

2 medium-sized quince, cored and quartered, not peeled

¼ cup (60 ml) petimezi / grape must syrup (see Note)

1 tbsp (15 ml) tomato paste

1 tsp garlic paste

1 tsp dried rosemary

1 tsp salt

½ tsp freshly ground black pepper

Mashed potatoes, to serve

In a large nonstick frying pan, heat 2 tablespoons (30 ml) of the olive oil over medium-high heat. Brown the meat on all sides for about 8 to 9 minutes, in batches if necessary, so as not to crowd the pan. Transfer the browned meat to a plate. Turn the heat to medium, add the onions to the pan and cook until translucent and fragrant, stirring often, for about 3 to 4 minutes. Put the meat and any juice that has accumulated on the plate back into the pan, turn the heat up and pour in the vinegar. Let it bubble for about 30 seconds before transferring everything, including the juices from the pan, to the slow cooker.

Place the quartered quince, skin side up, on top of the meat.

Mix the grape must syrup with the tomato paste, garlic paste, rosemary, salt and pepper, and pour over the contents of the slow cooker. Drizzle in the remaining 2 tablespoons (30 ml) of olive oil and cook on low for 6 to 8 hours or until the meat is fall-apart tender.

Although not quite traditional, mashed potato is the best accompaniment to this dish, as it helps collect every last drop of the delicious gravy.

Note: You can find grape must syrup (also known as grape must molasses) online or in Greek delicatessens. Pomegranate molasses can be used in its place, although the taste will be milder, so it's well worth looking for the petimezi.

Festive Pork Knuckle in Orange and Beer Sauce

(HIRINO KOTSI)

Pork knuckles are an inexpensive cut of meat and benefit from extended cooking at a low temperature. What better way than to cook them in a slow cooker!

Presenting a couple of big, golden pork knuckles on your festive dinner table is a great way to impress guests. They are more bone than meat, so two knuckles can either be served as a main course for up to four people, or featured in a buffet spread along with other main dishes. They aren't only for parties, though; pork knuckles can be a great *mezze*, or appetizer, for a friendly gathering such as Super Bowl Sunday or Oscar Night. Don't forget the cold beer!

1⅓ cups (170 g) carrots, sliced to ¼-inch (6-mm) thickness

1 cup (110 g) sliced onion

½ cup (120 ml) prepared yellow mustard

¼ cup (60 ml) honey

1 tbsp (15 ml) garlic paste

1 tsp salt

½ tsp freshly ground black pepper

1 tsp sweet paprika

1 tsp dried rosemary

2 large (3½-lb [1.6-kg]) fresh pork knuckles, unsmoked, uncured, skin on

½ cup (120 ml) freshly squeezed orange juice

½ cup (120 ml) mild beer (such as lager)

Sweet and regular roasted potatoes, to serve

In the bottom of the slow cooker insert, combine the carrots and onion.

Mix the mustard, honey, garlic paste, salt, black pepper, paprika and rosemary in a small bowl. Slather the mixture all over the two pieces of meat. Place them in the slow cooker. It will be very full!

Carefully pour the orange juice and beer around the pork. Cook on low for 7 to 8 hours, or until the meat is falling off the bone.

If desired, transfer the knuckles to a baking tray lined with grease-proof paper, and broil them for 5 to 8 minutes, or until they start to color. Be careful as the skin might start "spitting."

Blend the carrots, onion and cooking juices with an immersion blender and serve as a sauce for the meat. Serve with roasted sweet and regular potatoes.

Cumin-Spiced Meatballs in Rich Tomato Sauce

(SOUTZOUKAKIA)

Soutzoukakia is a dish of Turkish origin, brought over by the Greek refugees of Asia Minor in the early 1900s. The word soutzoukakia is a combination of the Turkish word *sucuk*, which means sausage, and the Greek diminutive *-akia*, translating to "little sausages," something their oblong shape is indeed reminiscent of.

Apart from their odd shape, what makes soutzoukakia different from other meatballs is the liberal use of garlic in their preparation and their distinct aroma of cumin. Some versions also have a hint of cinnamon hiding in the background. Two teaspoons (10 g) worth of mild garlic paste in this recipe could be considered lightweight to some, so I must admit I let my personal preference interfere. Feel free to load up on more, or use minced garlic for a stronger taste, if that is your thing.

For the meatballs

1 cup (100 g) bread crumbs, tightly packed (about 3 slices of stale bread—I use multigrain)

¼ cup (60 ml) red wine

1½ lb (680 g) ground beef

2 tsp (10 g) mild garlic paste, or 1–2 minced cloves garlic

1 tbsp (2 g) dried parsley

¾ tsp salt

1½ tsp (3 g) powdered cumin

¼ tsp black pepper

¼ tsp cinnamon

For the sauce

1 (28-oz [794-g]) can diced tomatoes, no salt added, with liquid

1 tbsp (15 g) butter

2 tsp (2 g) dried onion flakes, or 1 tsp onion powder

½ tsp salt

½ tsp sugar

½ tsp sweet paprika

Rice, mashed potatoes or French fries, to serve

Toss the bread crumbs with the red wine in a small bowl using your fingers. They won't become very wet.

Place the ground beef in a large bowl. Add the moist bread crumbs, garlic paste, parsley, salt, cumin, black pepper and cinnamon. Using your hands, knead the mixture well for 4 to 5 minutes, then let it rest for about 10 minutes.

Stir all the ingredients for the sauce in the slow cooker insert.

Shape 3 level tablespoons of the mixture into long, oval-shaped meatballs. You should get about sixteen meatballs. Place them on top of the sauce in the slow cooker without mixing. Cook on low for 6 to 7 hours, or until the meatballs are fully cooked and the sauce is slightly thickened. They can be stirred or flipped gently toward the end of cooking if desired.

Serve over rice or mashed potatoes or home-cooked French fries, with a generous helping of sauce.

Lamb Fricassee with Lettuce and Chard

(ARNAKI FRIKASE)

SERVES 4—6

You may be familiar with the word *fricassee*, but in Greek cooking it means something slightly different. In Greece, when you hear fricassee, you more often than not get a stew with greens, herbs and egg-lemon sauce (avgolemono). Lamb is a classic choice for Greek fricassee, and here I chose to add some chard to complement the usual lettuce.

A Greek cookbook would be very much incomplete without a lamb recipe or two, and although I am not a huge fan of lamb, even I can attest to the perfect result in texture that the slow cooker achieves with this somewhat difficult meat. And my testers can attest to the perfection of its flavor!

⅔ cup (85 g) spring onions, finely chopped, tightly packed

4½ oz (130 g) chard, chopped into large pieces (see Note)

½ cup (30 g) finely chopped dill, tightly packed

8 oz (225 g) Romaine lettuce, chopped into large pieces

2½ lb (1.1 kg) boneless leg of lamb, cut into large pieces

⅓ cup (45 g) flour for dredging, lightly packed

¼ cup (60 ml) olive oil, divided

1 tsp salt

½ tsp lemon pepper

¼ tsp sugar

1½ cups (360 ml) hot chicken stock

1 egg

¼ cup (60 ml) freshly squeezed lemon juice

Fresh crusty bread, to serve

Place the spring onions, chard, dill and Romaine in the slow cooker insert.

Prepare the meat by cutting off any fatty bits. Dredge all sides of each piece through the flour, shake off the excess and set aside on a clean plate. Discard the leftover flour.

Heat 1 or 2 tablespoons (15 or 30 ml) of the olive oil in a large frying pan over medium-high. (Use 1 tablespoon [15 ml] per batch if you think you will have to sear the meat in two lots; two if it all fits in your pan without being overcrowded.) Cook for about 5 minutes, turning frequently, until the meat is nicely browned on all sides. Place the lamb on the bed of greens in the slow cooker.

Stir the salt, lemon pepper and sugar into the hot chicken stock and pour over the meat and greens. Drizzle with the remaining 2 tablespoons (30 ml) of olive oil.

Cook on low for 7 to 8 hours or until the meat is tender and the chard stalks are very soft when you pinch them with your fingers.

In a medium-sized bowl, beat the egg with a stick blender while slowly adding the lemon juice. Turn the slow cooker off and bring the bowl next to it. Using a measuring cup or ladle, gradually transfer small quantities of the hot cooking liquid to the egg-lemon mixture, starting with about 1 tablespoon (15 ml) at a time. Increase the quantity of liquid that you are transferring as the mixture gets warmer. When the bowl is quite full and hot to the touch, pour the mixture back into the slow cooker. Lift the appliance by the handles and move it in a circular motion so the sauce is nicely distributed. Put the lid on and let the food rest for 5 minutes before serving.

Enjoy with fresh crusty bread to mop up the lovely sauce.

Note: For the chard in this recipe, you can use either baby chard with small stalks or large leaves without stalks.

Greek Stuffed Meatloaf

(ROLO KIMA)

This dish gives me a real '80s feeling, although I'm not sure when it first appeared in Greece. It may have been well before that, as it has quite a retro air to it, especially the version with boiled eggs in the middle. It was once a very popular dinner party dish and appeared often on many family Sunday tables. Today it's one of those meals that you don't frequently think of making, but when you do you wonder why on earth it's not on your monthly meal plan. Well, I hope the ease with which it can be prepared in the slow cooker makes you think of it more often.

In terms of the filling, I took a different route for my meatloaf to the classic boiled eggs, with the slightly Greek-ier flavors of yellow cheese and roasted red peppers.

2 lb (900 g) ground beef

¾ cup (85 g) wheat rusks processed into very fine crumbs, tightly packed (see Note)

¾ cup (140 g) minced onion, lightly packed

2 eggs

2 tbsp (30 ml) Worcestershire sauce

1 tbsp (15 ml) balsamic vinegar

1 tbsp (2 g) dried parsley

1½ tsp (9 g) salt

1½ tsp (9 g) dried oregano

½–1 tsp black pepper

1 tsp sweet paprika

For the potatoes

2½ lb (1.1 kg) baby potatoes, skin on, scrubbed

2 tbsp (30 ml) olive oil

¼ tsp salt

For the filling

4½ oz (130 g) roasted red peppers (from a jar), cut into strips

3 oz (85 g) Cretan Gruyère or kasseri cheese, cut into sticks

Yellow mustard, to serve

In a large bowl, mix the ground beef with the wheat rusks, onion, eggs, Worcestershire sauce, vinegar, parsley, salt, oregano, pepper and paprika. Knead well with your hands for 5 minutes and refrigerate for at least half an hour.

Place the potatoes in the bottom of the slow cooker, drizzle with the olive oil and sprinkle with the salt. Toss with your fingers to coat.

Lay a large piece of parchment paper on a clean work surface and empty the meat mixture on top. Shape into a rectangle (about 10 x 11 inches [25 x 28 cm]). Place the red peppers and cheese sticks along the length of the rectangle in the middle and bring the long sides of the paper up to meet on top. Pinch and press the ground meat with your fingers so it seals into a roll. Be sure to do this carefully and diligently so the seal doesn't open up during cooking.

Gently transfer the meat roll—seal side down—on top of the potatoes. Cook on low for 7 to 8 hours, or until a food thermometer reads at least 160°F (71°C).

Let the meat roll rest for a while before removing it from the slow cooker (you might find it easiest to use your hands to lift it). Cover with foil to keep warm and let it rest a little more before slicing.

Serve with the potatoes and some prepared yellow mustard on the side.

Note: Wheat rusks can be found online or at Greek delis. They are called frigania or friganies in Greek. You might see them called thin white rusks, thin wheat rusks or golden rusks. They are like small slices of crunchy, dry toast in appearance and can be eaten as is. They are different from the very tough rusks called paximadia. Although the wheat rusks are ideal for this recipe, unseasoned panko is a good alternative (use 1⅓ cups [85 g]) and there are also some Italian brands of rusks which would work too.

Pork and Celery Stew

(HIRINO SELINO)

A true classic, pork and celery is one of Greece's beloved dishes. Visitors to Greece may not be familiar with it, as it's usually made in winter due to the seasonality of some of its ingredients. In some areas, *Hirino Selino* is actually a festive dish enjoyed at Christmas.

Typical celery in Greece is quite different to that found in northern Europe and the U.S. It has very thin long stalks and lots of dark green leaves that look similar to flat parsley. I've always called it Greek celery as I didn't know it was available elsewhere. With a bit of research, I discovered that in fact this type is called Chinese celery, or leaf celery. However, since it doesn't seem to be easily accessible, I've used the more common thick celery in this recipe. Just make sure you get a bunch or two that still have the top part attached, with the thinner ribs and leaves; this is the part we'll use. Keep the rest for another use, like maybe a nice Waldorf salad.

---

1 lb (450 g) celery tops (thin ribs with leaves)

¾ cup (110 g) finely chopped onion, lightly packed

⅓ lb (140 g) leek, sliced into 1½-inch (4-cm) tubes

¼ cup (60 ml) olive oil, divided

2 lb (900 g) pork neck or Boston butt, cut into 4 large chunks (see Note)

1 tsp salt

½ tsp lemon pepper

1½ cups (360 ml) hot chicken stock

2 eggs

¼ cup (60 ml) freshly squeezed lemon juice

Fresh bread, to serve

Remove the leaves from the thin celery ribs (you can do this quickly with your fingers), then chop the ribs into pieces approximately 1 to 1½ inches (2.5 to 4 cm) long.

Place the celery ribs, onion and leek in the slow cooker insert and drizzle with 1 tablespoon (15 ml) of the olive oil. Mix well.

Add the celery leaves on top and nestle the meat among them.

Sprinkle with the salt and lemon pepper, and pour the chicken stock over everything. Drizzle with the remaining 3 tablespoons (45 ml) of olive oil.

Cook on low for 7 to 9 hours, or until the meat is tender and the celery is soft. If you can, push the celery leaves down into the liquid a couple hours before the end of the cooking time.

Turn the slow cooker off. In a medium-sized bowl, beat the eggs while slowly adding the lemon juice. Bring the bowl next to the slow cooker and carefully start spooning hot cooking liquid into the eggs while continuously beating them. A ½-cup (120-ml) measuring cup works well for this. Start with a tablespoon (15 ml) and gradually increase the amount until you are transferring ½ cup (120 ml) at a time. When you have transferred most of the liquid and the bowl feels hot to the touch, pour the egg mixture back into the slow cooker insert. Hold the cooker by the side handles and move it in a circular motion to get the sauce well distributed. Replace the lid and let the pork rest for a few minutes.

Serve with fresh bread.

Note: While the pork neck cut works beautifully for this recipe, you can substitute with the Boston butt or your own favorite cut of pork for slow cooking.

Beef and Rice Meatballs in Egg-Lemon Soup

(GIOUVARLAKIA SOUPA)

Mention the word *giouvarlakia* to any Greek and they will start daydreaming of their mother's cooking. I would even go as far as saying that it's on our top-ten list of comfort foods. Tasty meat and rice balls, floating in a tangy egg-lemon soup—what's not to love? The ingredients are simple but come together beautifully to make a delicious and filling dish.

There are two main versions of giouvarlakia. In one, the meatballs are in a soup; in the other they are smothered in a thick egg-lemon sauce. The only real difference is the quantity of liquid used to cook them. Traditional recipes use water instead of stock, but modern ones often provide that extra boost of flavor. Tarragon is a rarer addition but suits this dish perfectly.

4 cups (960 ml) hot vegetable stock

4 cups (960 ml) cold tap water

1 tbsp (15 g) butter

1¾ tsp (11 g) salt, divided

2 lb (900 g) ground beef, or a mix of ground beef and pork

½ cup (85 g) arborio rice

¾ cup (140 g) minced onion, lightly packed

¼ cup (15 g) finely chopped parsley leaves, tightly packed

1 tsp dried tarragon

1 tbsp (15 ml) olive oil

½ tsp black pepper

2 eggs

5 tbsp (75 ml) freshly squeezed lemon juice

Freshly ground black pepper, to serve

Fresh crusty bread, to serve

Feta cheese, to serve

Pour the hot vegetable stock and the water into the slow cooker, and add the butter and ¼ teaspoon of the salt.

In a large mixing bowl, combine the beef, rice, onion, parsley, tarragon, oil, the remaining 1½ teaspoons (9 g) of salt and the pepper. Mix well with your hands, kneading lightly for a couple of minutes.

Take 3 level tablespoons of the mixture and shape it into a large meatball. Set aside on a plate. Continue with the rest of the mixture and then gently drop all the meatballs into the slow cooker. There should be about 22 balls.

Cook on low for 5 to 6 hours, or until the meatballs are cooked through. Turn the slow cooker off.

In a medium-sized mixing bowl, beat the eggs and lemon juice until well combined. Place the bowl next to the slow cooker, and use a ladle or measuring cup to slowly add small amounts of hot soup into the egg mixture, beating continuously. Start with about 1 tablespoon (15 ml) at a time, and gradually increase the amount of soup added to the bowl. When at least 2 to 3 cups (480 to 720 ml) of soup have been transferred to the egg mixture, and the bowl feels hot to the touch, pour the mixture back into the insert while stirring gently.

Serve the soup with freshly ground black pepper, fresh crusty bread and feta cheese.

White Wine–Braised Pork with Peppers and Mushrooms

(HIRINO KRASSATO)

In all honesty, it would be a little far-fetched to call this a classic Greek recipe. It's more of a contemporary take on the traditional *krassato* dishes, but it is something a modern Greek might easily choose to cook at home. Krassato means "with wine," and the classic versions are very tasty, but have fewer ingredients. They wouldn't, for example, include mushrooms and peppers. Nowadays, Greeks are a lot more adventurous in their cooking, so we're deviating from the classics a little and painting a more complete picture of what one might find on a modern Greek dinner table.

5 tbsp (75 ml) olive oil, divided

¾ cup (110 g) finely chopped onion, lightly packed

1 tsp minced garlic

1 large red bell pepper, sliced into rounds

1 large yellow bell pepper, sliced into rounds

1 (8-oz [225-g]) package pre-sliced white mushrooms

2 lb (900 g) boneless pork neck or Boston pork butt, cut into large chunks (see note)

½ cup (120 ml) white wine

2 tbsp (30 ml) white balsamic vinegar

1 tbsp (15 ml) prepared yellow mustard

1 tsp thyme

1 tsp salt

½ tsp powdered coriander

½ tsp sweet paprika

¼ tsp freshly ground black pepper

French fries, mashed potatoes or crusty bread, to serve

Heat 1 tablespoon (15 ml) of the olive oil in a large nonstick frying pan over medium heat. Add the onions and cook gently until they become translucent and start to soften, about 5 minutes. Add the garlic and continue cooking for another 30 seconds to a minute, stirring continuously. Transfer the contents of the pan to the slow cooker insert.

Add 2 tablespoons (30 ml) of the olive oil to the same pan, still over medium heat. Add the bell peppers and cook until they start to soften, for about 7 to 9 minutes. Remove the bell peppers with a slotted spoon and transfer them to the slow cooker.

Add the mushrooms to the pan (there should still be some oil there) and cook until they are brown and all their juices have evaporated, about 6 to 8 minutes. Tip the mushrooms into the slow cooker.

Turn the stove to medium-high and pour the remaining 2 tablespoons (30 ml) of oil into the pan. Add the pork and brown on all sides, cooking for about 8 minutes. Do this in batches if necessary, so that the meat is not crowded. Place the pieces of meat on top of the vegetables in the slow cooker.

While the frying pan is still hot, pour in the wine and white balsamic vinegar. Let the liquid bubble for a few seconds and tip it into the slow cooker. Add the mustard (you can dollop some onto each piece of meat), and sprinkle in the thyme, salt, coriander, paprika and pepper.

Cook on low for 6 to 7 hours, or until the meat is fall-apart tender. You can flip the meat over during cooking if desired.

Serve with French fries, mashed potatoes or a good crusty bread.

Note: I've had best results with the pork neck for this dish, but the Boston butt or your own favorite cut of pork for slow cooking can be substituted as well.

Lamb in Zesty Lemon Sauce

(ARNAKI LEMONATO)

Lamb or goat in the oven with potatoes is extremely popular in Greece and is often served on special occasions. In the not so distant past, it would be common practice to prepare the ingredients in a large baking tin and take it to the local bakery to be cooked in the huge ovens. It's not such a frequent event now, but it's not unheard of, especially around the holidays. The sight of someone leaving the bakery with a big *tapsi* (baking dish), maybe pinching a potato from under the tin foil while hurrying home, conjures up very fond childhood memories.

Bakery ovens and fond memories are all very well, but when cooking at home, it's important to use a fail-proof method. And the best way to achieve a beautifully cooked shoulder of lamb is definitely in a slow cooker. It won't give the color that an oven will, but in terms of moistness, flavor and ease, it can't be beat.

---

2 lb (900 g) peeled potatoes, cut into medium-size pieces

1 cup (140 g) sliced carrots

5 tbsp (75 ml) freshly squeezed lemon juice, divided

2 tbsp (30 ml) olive oil

2 tbsp (30 ml) prepared yellow mustard

2 tsp (10 g) mild garlic paste

2 tsp (2.5 g) dried rosemary

½ tsp sumac (see Notes)

1 tsp salt

¼ tsp freshly ground black pepper

3 lb (1.4 kg) lamb shoulder, bone in, cut into large portions (see Notes)

2 medium onions, halved or quartered

Place the potatoes and carrots in the bottom of the slow cooker.

In a clean jar, combine 1 tablespoon (15 ml) of the lemon juice, the oil, mustard, garlic paste, rosemary, sumac, salt and pepper. Put the lid on and shake well.

Trim the excess fat off the meat and smother it with the lemon juice mixture. Place it on top of the potatoes in the slow cooker.

Rinse the jar out with the 4 tablespoons (60 ml) of lemon juice and pour it around the meat. Place the onions on or around the lamb.

Cook on low for 6 to 7 hours, or until the potatoes are tender and the meat is falling off the bone.

Serve the lamb, potatoes and carrots with a drizzle of the cooking juices.

Notes: Sumac is a spice found in Middle Eastern delis, and can also be ordered online.

The lamb shoulder should be 3 pounds (1.4 kg) in total. Ask your butcher to cut it and explain that you want the meat off the bone to come to about 2 pounds (900 g).

Aromatic Beef in Spiced Wine Sauce with Bucatini Pasta

(PASTITSADA)

Pastitsada, a famous dish from the island of Corfu, has suffered many modifications over the years. A quick search on the Internet will produce numerous recipes, many of which are tomato based. The original, however, didn't have any tomatoes, in any form. I too have deviated from the original, but only slightly, adding a bit of tomato paste mainly for its depth of flavor and umami.

The dish is heavily spiced, with warm "autumn" spices such as cinnamon, allspice and cloves. Wine and vinegar play a major role in Pastitsada, resulting in beautifully tender meat and a very intense sauce that lightly coats the bucatini pasta, giving it a delicious flavor.

¼ cup (60 ml) olive oil, divided

1¼ cups (170 g) finely chopped onion, lightly packed

2 tbsp (14 g) sweet paprika

1 tsp cinnamon

1 tsp sugar

1 tsp salt

½ tsp powdered allspice

¼ tsp freshly ground black pepper

¼ tsp powdered nutmeg

⅛ tsp powdered cloves

2 lb (900 g) beef shank, boneless, in large chunks

¼ cup (60 ml) good-quality red wine vinegar

¾ cup (180 ml) good-quality red wine

1 tbsp (15 ml) tomato paste

2 tsp (10 g) garlic paste

2 bay leaves

1 lb (450 g) bucatini pasta

Grated kefalotyri, to serve

Heat 2 tablespoons (30 ml) of the olive oil over medium heat in a large nonstick frying pan. Add the onion, stir and let it cook for about 10 minutes, without letting it brown too much.

While the onion is cooking, measure out the paprika, cinnamon, sugar, salt, allspice, black pepper, nutmeg and cloves into a small container.

Tip the cooked onion into the slow cooker and return the pan to the stove. Add 2 tablespoons (30 ml) of the olive oil to the pan and turn the heat up to medium-high. Brown the meat on all sides for about 7 to 9 minutes. Do this in batches if necessary, so everything isn't crowded in the pan. Remove the meat with kitchen tongs and place it in the slow cooker insert.

Pour the vinegar and wine into the hot pan and let it bubble for a few seconds while scraping the bottom. Take the pan off the heat. Add the tomato and garlic pastes, stir to incorporate and then add the spice mixture. Stir well and pour everything onto the meat. Scrape the bottom with a flat cooking utensil to get all the spices.

Add the bay leaves and cook on low for 5 to 6 hours, or until the meat is tender and the sauce is slightly thickened.

Just before the end, cook the pasta in a separate pot according to the package instructions.

Turn the slow cooker off, remove the cooked beef with tongs and set aside. Remove and discard the bay leaves, then blitz the sauce with a stick blender until smooth. Add the cooked pasta to the sauce in the pot, toss to coat and serve with a piece of beef and a generous sprinkling of grated kefalotyri.

Note: This recipe doesn't yield a large amount of sauce. This is fine, since the taste is strong and ideally it should just coat the pasta.

Beef in Garlicky Parsley and Wine Sauce

(SOFRITO)

Another famous dish from Corfu. Don't be confused by the name: in international cooking terms it means a sauce or puree made with vegetables and used as a base for other dishes. It's mainly used in Italian, Spanish, Portuguese and Latin American cuisines. In Greek, however, *Sofrito* is the name of this intensely flavorful meal.

Traditionally, Sofrito is made with thin slices from the cut of beef known here as *keeloto*, which is the rump or top part of the round. This cut wouldn't work in the slow cooker, so I've switched to a cut which does: the "osso bucco" (i.e., crosscut shank). It may look very different from the original with these thick pieces of beef, but the important thing is to achieve a nicely cooked and tender result. As with all the meat dishes, I suggest you use your favorite cut.

2 lb (900 g) beef crosscut shank, or any beef steaks suitable for slow cooking

⅓ cup (40 g) flour, lightly packed

2½ cups (85 g) parsley leaves, roughly chopped, tightly packed

5 tbsp (75 ml) olive oil, divided

2 tsp (5 g) minced garlic

¼ cup (60 ml) white balsamic vinegar

½ cup (120 ml) white wine

½ cup (120 ml) hot beef stock

1 tsp salt

½ tsp freshly ground black pepper

Mashed potatoes or homemade, thickly cut French fries, to serve

Dredge the steaks in the flour, dust off any excess and set aside.

Place the parsley in the bottom of the slow cooker.

Heat 1 tablespoon (15 ml) of the olive oil in a large nonstick frying pan over medium-low heat and gently cook the garlic for about 30 seconds, or until golden and fragrant. Transfer the garlic to the slow cooker insert.

Add 2 tablespoons (30 ml) of the olive oil to the pan, turn the heat to medium-high and sauté the beef until it has a nice brown color on all sides, about 8 minutes. Do this in batches if necessary, so as not to crowd the meat in the pan, splitting the oil between batches. Place the beef on top of the parsley in the slow cooker.

While the pan is hot, pour in the vinegar, wine and beef stock to deglaze it, scraping up any pieces of meat stuck to the bottom. Let the liquid bubble for 10 to 15 seconds and pour over the meat. Sprinkle with the salt and pepper and drizzle in the 2 remaining tablespoons (30 ml) of olive oil.

Cook on low for 5 to 7 hours, or until the beef is tender and falling apart.

Serve with the sauce from the pot and a side of mashed potatoes or homemade French fries.

Spicy Country-Style Beef Sausages with Mixed Bell Peppers

(SPETZOFAI)

SERVES 4—6

Greek country-style sausages are quite unique. They are usually heavy on the herbs and often contain fennel, orange and/or leeks. Although very tasty, they can be quite tough and fatty. One of the great surprises the slow cooker had in store for me was the perfect way it cooks Greek sausage. I was truly amazed the first time I tried it. Soft, flavorful and without a trace of those pesky fatty bits that can sometimes ruin an otherwise perfect mouthful. They just melt away with the extended cooking. That probably explains the deliciousness of the sauce they produce!

Here they are combined with bell peppers to make *Spetzofai*, a great mezze-type dish. Most versions use pork sausages, which are the most common in Greece. While researching the recipe, however, I found that the original Spetzofai may have used beef or lamb sausage, or a mix. I won't swear by the information, as it's hard to find reputable sources for this sort of thing, but I did like the idea of using beef here instead of pork, so it suits me just fine.

¾ cup (110 g) finely chopped onion, lightly packed

2 lb (900 g) Greek country-style beef sausages, sliced (see Note)

¼ cup (60 ml) tomato paste

1 medium yellow bell pepper, cut in thick slices (about ¾-inch [2-cm])

1 medium green bell pepper, cut in thick slices (about ¾-inch [2-cm])

2 medium red bell peppers, cut in thick slices (about ¾-inch [2-cm])

1 tsp oregano

1 tsp sugar

½ tsp salt

¼ tsp black pepper

2 tbsp (30 ml) olive oil

Fresh bread and feta, to serve

Place the onion and sausages in the slow cooker insert. Add the tomato paste and stir well to distribute it. Put the sliced bell peppers on top.

Sprinkle with the oregano, sugar, salt and black pepper, and drizzle with the olive oil.

Cook on low for 3½ to 4½ hours until the bell peppers are soft and the sausages are cooked through. Then prop the lid open with the handle of a wooden spoon, and cook for 1 hour longer to thicken the sauce a little.

Serve either warm (not hot) or at room temperature, as a mezze or a main meal. It is, of course, great with fresh bread and feta.

Note: Look for raw Greek beef or pork sausages or "loukaniko" at Mediterranean markets or online. If you can't find them, you could use raw Italian-style sausage (preferably with fennel) but the result might be slightly different.

Stuffed Zucchini in Thick Egg-Lemon Sauce

(KOLOKYTHAKIA GEMISTA)

Are you familiar with the term *gemista*? If so, you might think it means stuffed tomatoes, since it usually does refer to them when used on its own. However, the word actually just means "stuffed," so it can refer to anything. Well, anything with a stuffing! Here we have the classic Greek dish of stuffed zucchini smothered in an egg-lemon sauce, one of my childhood favorites. This might be a meat dish but the amount of actual ground meat used is very little, thus it's one of those frugal meals that "make a little go a long way."

Hollowing out the zucchini might seem a bit fussy, but once you get the hang of it it's not at all hard to do. And the result is definitely worth it!

---

8 large (8-oz [225 g]) zucchini with ends removed

9 oz (255 g) peeled potato, cut into medium-sized pieces

1 cup (140 g) sliced carrots

1 tsp salt, divided

⅓ lb (150 g) ground beef

¼ lb (110 g) ground pork

½ cup (110 g) minced onion, tightly packed

½ cup (85 g) arborio rice

¼ cup (15 g) finely chopped parsley leaves, tightly packed

¼ cup (15 g) finely chopped dill leaves, tightly packed

6 tbsp (90 ml) olive oil, divided

¼ tsp black pepper

½ tsp dried thyme

1½ cups (360 ml) hot vegetable or chicken stock

2 eggs

¼ cup (60 ml) freshly squeezed lemon juice

Fresh crusty bread and feta, to serve

Using a straight vegetable peeler, carefully hollow out the flesh of the zucchini, working from both sides. Don't remove too much flesh, so the zucchini "shells" aren't too soft. Set the zucchini aside and store the flesh for another use.

Place the potato and carrots at the bottom of the slow cooker insert and sprinkle them with ¼ teaspoon of salt.

Combine the ground beef, ground pork, onion, rice, parsley, dill, 3 tablespoons (45 ml) of the olive oil, the remaining salt, pepper and thyme in a large bowl. Toss well with your hands, without kneading the mixture.

Stuff each zucchini with the filling, pressing it down into the center and leaving a little space at each end for the rice to expand. Place the stuffed zucchini on top of the potatoes and carrots.

Drizzle the zucchini and vegetables with the remaining 3 tablespoons (45 ml) of the olive oil and add the vegetable or chicken stock to the slow cooker (it won't cover the zucchini).

Cook on low for 5 to 6 hours, or until the meat and rice are fully cooked through and the potatoes are tender.

When ready, turn off the slow cooker and bring a medium-size bowl next to it. Beat the eggs with the lemon juice in the bowl and start adding hot liquid from the slow cooker, slowly and in small quantities to begin with, while beating continuously. Using a stick blender for this is a good idea as it will help thicken the sauce. As the mixture in the bowl gets warmer, increase the quantities of cooking liquid you add to it (tilt the slow cooker to help with this). When most of the cooking liquid has been transferred to the egg-lemon mixture, and the bowl is hot to the touch, pour the sauce back into the insert over the zucchini. Move the slow cooker, holding it by the side handles, in circular movements so the sauce is distributed evenly and let it rest with the lid on for a few minutes before serving.

Serve with lots of fresh crusty bread and feta cheese.

Spaghetti and Greek Meat Sauce

(MAKARONIA ME KIMA)

Another contender for the top-ten comfort foods list. If you ask Greeks what their favorite food is, *Makaronia me Kima* is what you'll hear from a large proportion of the population. Loved by adults and children alike, spaghetti with meat sauce may not be a traditional Greek dish, but it has a special place in our hearts.

Most versions of meat sauce in Greece don't have vegetables; just a little bit of onion, the meat, tomato of course, and spices such as cinnamon and allspice. Adding carrot, however, is a good trick to give a little sweetness and it's not unheard of here. Apart from the sweetness, it also bulks up the recipe, making it more frugal and healthier in one go. Can't argue with that, can we? I take it a step further and also add red bell pepper.

Note the trick of putting cheese on the plate before adding the pasta! I can't say for sure it's a custom of Greek origin, but it's something we do here, especially with Makaronia me Kima!

¼ cup (60 ml) olive oil, divided

1¼ cups (170 g) finely chopped onion, lightly packed

1½ cups (200 g) finely chopped red bell peppers

1⅓ cups (170 g) coarsely grated carrot, tightly packed

1¾ lb (800 g) ground beef (not too lean)

¼ cup (60 ml) balsamic vinegar

2 tbsp (30 ml) tomato paste

2 tsp (10 g) mild garlic paste

1½ tsp (9 g) salt

½ tsp freshly ground black pepper

¼ tsp sugar

¼ tsp allspice

½ tsp cinnamon

1 (28-oz [794-g]) can diced tomatoes, no salt added, with liquid

2 bay leaves

1 lb (450 g) spaghetti

Hard mizithra cheese, grated, to serve

Heat 1 tablespoon (15 ml) of the olive oil in a large nonstick frying pan over medium heat. Gently cook the onions and bell peppers for about 10 minutes, or until the onions are golden and the bell peppers have started to soften. Transfer them to the slow cooker insert.

Add 1 more tablespoon (15 ml) of the olive oil to the pan, then add the carrots and cook for about 5 minutes, until softened (the pan will be dry). Tip them into the slow cooker with the onion.

Turn the heat to medium-high, add another tablespoon (15 ml) of the olive oil to the pan and then add the ground beef. Break it up with a wooden spoon and cook while stirring almost continuously to avoid lumps. It will release its juices and then dry out. When the meat starts to make a sizzling noise in the pan, after about 8 minutes in total, add the balsamic vinegar and stir well for one more minute. Tip it all into the slow cooker.

Add the tomato paste, garlic paste, salt, pepper, sugar, allspice, cinnamon and tomatoes. Drizzle the last tablespoon (15 ml) of olive oil over the top and add the bay leaves. Stir gently and cook on low for 7 to 8 hours, or until the sauce reaches the consistency you prefer. Keep in mind that the longer it cooks, the better it tastes. If it turns out too thick for your liking, add ½ cup (120 ml) of hot water and let it cook for another 30 minutes.

Just before serving, boil the spaghetti according to the instructions on the package and drain it well. Remove the bay leaves from the sauce and discard. Sprinkle some mizithra cheese onto the plates, divide the spaghetti between them, add sauce on top and sprinkle with more cheese.

Succulent Pork Chops with Beer Mustard Sauce and Potatoes

(BRIZOLES ME PATATES)

Pork chops are tricky. At least, Greek pork chops are. They aren't the easiest to get right as they can dry out really quickly while cooking. The most popular way to eat them is in a *taverna* (restaurant), grilled over charcoal. At home though, nothing beats the slow cooker for making tasty, succulent pork chops.

This is another modern-style recipe, as beer wasn't traditionally used in cooking. It suits the chops very well, and the red bell peppers and capers add to the unique flavor.

---

2 lb (900 g) peeled potatoes, cut into medium-small pieces

1 tsp salt, divided

4 (½ lb [225 g]) pork neck or shoulder/blade chops (see Note)

2 small red bell peppers, cut into thick 1-inch (2-cm) strips

2 tbsp (30 ml) Dijon mustard

2 tbsp (30 g) brown sugar

1 tsp dried savory (the herb), or dried thyme

¾ cup (180 ml) beer, such as an IPA

2 tbsp (30 ml) capers preserved in brine, rinsed

2 small onions, halved

2 tbsp (30 ml) olive oil

Put the potatoes in the bottom of the slow cooker insert and sprinkle them with ¼ teaspoon of salt. Lay the pork chops on top, trying to keep them in one layer if possible, but it is fine if they overlap. Top the chops with the red bell peppers.

Stir the mustard, brown sugar, savory and ¾ teaspoon of salt into the beer until the mustard is dissolved. Pour the mixture over the contents of the slow cooker.

Sprinkle the capers over the pork chops and place one onion half on each chop, cut side down. Drizzle with the olive oil.

Cook on low for 4 to 6 hours, or until the pork chops are tender and the potatoes are soft. Cooking time will largely depend on the thickness of the pork chops. Cut the potatoes accordingly; if the chops are thick, cut the potatoes into medium pieces, and if the chops are thin, cut them into smaller pieces.

Serve the pork chops, bell peppers and potatoes with a drizzle of some of the cooking juices.

Note: If you don't like or can't find pork neck or shoulder chops, you can use your favorite cut for slow cooking. Alternatively, you can use a less fatty cut, but keep in mind the meat might dry out a bit during cooking. A good solution is to leave out the potatoes and cook the chops submerged in the liquid. Make mashed potatoes on the stovetop and serve with those instead.

Country-Style Sausage Pasta Sauce

(SALTSA ME LOUKANIKO)

This recipe is, for me, the ultimate weeknight meal. It may be the easiest one in the book, with few ingredients but so much wonderful flavor.

Greek country-style sausages—we call them "village sausages"—tend to have lots of seasoning and herbs, so if you can find strong tasting ones you could probably even skip the extra ingredients and use only onion, tomato and a little sugar in the sauce.

The method is my all-time favorite: Add everything to the pot and cook. To call it effortless would be an understatement.

---

1 lb (450 g) Greek country-style pork sausages, sliced (see Notes)

½ cup (85 g) finely chopped onion, very tightly packed

1 (28-oz [794-g]) can diced tomatoes, no salt added, with liquid

½ tsp sweet paprika

½ tsp sugar

½ tsp salt

½ tsp oregano (or to taste)

¼ tsp black pepper (or to taste)

Cooked pasta, to serve

Greek Gruyère or feta cheese, to serve

Combine the sausages, onions, tomatoes, paprika, sugar, salt, oregano and pepper in the slow cooker insert and stir.

Cook on low for 5 to 6 hours, or until the sausage is cooked through and very tender. Thicken the sauce, if needed, by finishing it off with the lid propped slightly open for an extra 30 minutes.

Serve over cooked pasta with a generous sprinkling of grated Greek Gruyère or crumbled feta.

Notes: The sauce could cook for longer if your schedule requires it. Don't prop the lid open unless you know you will be turning it off shortly.

Look for raw Greek pork sausages or loukaniko sausages at Mediterranean markets or online. If you can't find them, you could use raw Italian-style sausage (preferably with fennel), but the result might be slightly different.

LET'S BE HONEST. Fish can be a little intimidating, can't it? It's one of those things that some shy away from, thinking it's too complicated to get right. Overcooked, rubbery fish is not enjoyable and it seems like you have a split second to take it out of the oven or off the grill before you've crossed that line and your juicy fish is ruined. That split second is extended to several minutes in the slow cooker, so you can try the fish, see how it's going and take it out without feeling like you're sprinting against time. Much less stressful, if you ask me! In fact, although you don't see many recipes for fish in the slow cooker, it's actually one of the best ways to make it. Besides, how could fish and seafood be absent from a Greek cookery book?

Shrimp is like fish, and it does need some attention while cooking, but octopus and calamari are even more accommodating and don't mind staying in the pot for a bit longer. It may surprise you, but "low and slow" is just as good a method as "hot and fast" for both fish and seafood.

I must say the recipes in this chapter make me quite proud. They are fairly unusual and the results are so good that the whole time I was developing and testing them, I felt really excited. I can't wait for you to try them!

Fish in Spicy Pepper Sauce

(BOURDETO)

Bourdeto is a fairly unique dish, as it's much spicier than your average Greek food. It originates from Corfu and isn't often served anywhere else unless it's home-cooked. The various takes on the basic recipe don't seem to have many significant alterations between them, except one: the use of tomato. This is the only major difference, with some cooks choosing recipes that use fresh tomatoes or paste in addition to the red pepper spice. Others maintain that "real" bourdeto gets its color solely from the spice, and tomato paste is used only by those who want to reduce the spiciness without losing the vibrant redness of the sauce. I chose to omit the tomato paste in my recipe, since I found the pepper sauce to be very interesting just as it is.

Amazingly, my version seems, to me, to be very spicy, even though I use much less cayenne pepper than many of the recipes I found during my research. Could it be the spiciest traditional Greek dish around?

2 tbsp (30 ml) olive oil

1 tsp mild garlic paste

1 large onion, sliced into rounds

2 tbsp (16 g) sweet paprika

2 tsp (4 g) cayenne pepper

½ tsp salt

¼ tsp black pepper

¼ cup (60 ml) hot water

2 (1-lb [454-g]) orata fish, cleaned, head and tail on (see Note)

2 tbsp (30 ml) freshly squeezed lemon juice, to serve

Crusty bread, to serve

Place the olive oil, garlic paste, onions, paprika, cayenne, salt and black pepper in the slow cooker insert. Add the hot water, stir and cook on high for 1 hour.

Lay the fish on top of the onion mixture side by side and cook (still on high) for 1 to 2 hours or until the fish flakes easily with a fork.

Remove the fish carefully and transfer to a platter. Stir the sauce and onions in the pot well and transfer to a serving bowl. Serve the fish with some sauce, onions and a drizzle of lemon juice. Don't forget some crusty bread to mop up the sauce.

Tip: This dish is also very good with hand-cut French fries.

Note: Bourdeto is usually made with scorpion fish. Although I haven't seen any versions with orata (also known as dorade, or gilthead sea bream), I used it because it's a very popular fish in general in Greece, and it's very tasty. Take a look online to find local suppliers, or feel free to experiment with your favorite type of fish.

Fisherman's Soup
(PSAROSOUPA)

The most famous Greek fish soup is called *Kakavia* and the original is made with only a handful of ingredients. In the old days when fishermen went out to sea, they would take along a pot, some olive oil, potatoes, onions and lemons. The smaller fish that got caught in their nets, if deemed unsuitable for selling, would be boiled with these supplies in seawater, producing a deliciously tasty soup. Over time, many different versions have emerged with more ingredients added, mostly vegetables. Thus, the broader term *Psarosoupa* (which translates to, well, "fish soup") is now more appropriate.

Psarosoupa is one of those soups that I rarely think of making, and when I do, I wonder why I don't make it more often. It's nutritious, heart-warming and so tasty! Nowadays, the availability of fish stock makes it very easy too, since there is no need to use a variety of whole fish for flavor. And the slow cooker just takes it to a whole new level of effortlessness.

1 lb (450 g) peeled potatoes, cut into medium pieces

2 small tomatoes, cut into medium pieces

1 large onion, roughly chopped

1 cup (140 g) sliced carrots

¾ cup (85 g) sliced celery

6 tbsp (90 ml) olive oil

5 tbsp (75 ml) freshly squeezed lemon juice, plus extra, to serve

½ tsp black pepper

½ tsp salt (or to taste, depending on your stock)

1 bay leaf

4 cups (960 ml) hot, good quality fish stock

2 cups (480 ml) hot water

1½ lb (680 g) perch fillet (or other favorite fish fillet)

Freshly ground black pepper, to serve

Crusty bread, to serve

Add the potatoes, tomatoes, onions, carrots, celery, olive oil, lemon juice, pepper, salt, bay leaf, fish stock and hot water to the slow cooker. Cook on low for 7 to 8 hours, or until the potatoes and carrots are very soft.

Remove and discard the bay leaf, then blend the soup with a stick blender until smooth. Try to do this as quickly as possible so as not to let the soup cool too much.

Add the fish fillets and cook for 20 to 30 minutes on low. The time will largely depend on the thickness of the fillets you use. Perch is thick and meaty, so it takes a bit longer than a thin fillet would. Check the fish toward the end of the cook time to avoid letting it overcook and turn rubbery. It should flake easily with a fork.

Serve with extra lemon juice, freshly ground black pepper and lots of crusty bread.

Note: The perch in Greece is Nile perch. Search online for suppliers or good alternatives if it's hard to find.

Mac and Octopus

(HTAPODI ME MAKARONAKI)

When it comes to Greek cooking, one of my mum's specialties, octopus with short macaroni, is one of the most memorable of my childhood. It's well loved all over Greece, but there is one day in particular when it features on nearly everyone's table. That day is Clean Monday, the first day of Lent, a holiday during which seafood is the star of the show, along with sesame *halva* and a delicious flat-shaped bread called *Lagana*.

Even if Mac and Octopus brings to mind spring feasts and holidays for most Greeks, it is still a tasty idea for a midweek dinner that might get you out of the proverbial rut.

2 lb (900 g) octopus, bought frozen and fully thawed, cleaned and cut into large pieces

½ cup (120 ml) red wine

1 cup (240 ml) tomato passata (see Notes)

¼ cup (60 ml) hot water

2 tbsp (30 ml) olive oil

½ tsp salt

¼ tsp black pepper

1 bay leaf

2¾ cups (660 ml) boiling water, plus extra if necessary

12 oz (340 g) short pasta, such as ditalini

Grated mizithra cheese, optional, to serve

Put the octopus in a large, cold, nonstick frying pan and heat it over high heat. It will begin to release its juices, which will then start to evaporate. This will take about 10 minutes or more, depending on the octopus. When the pan is almost dry, with about a tablespoon (15 ml) of liquid left, add the wine. Let it bubble for a few seconds while stirring, and tip everything into the slow cooker insert.

Pour the passata into the slow cooker and add the hot water, olive oil, salt, pepper and bay leaf.

Cook on low for 7 to 8 hours, or until the octopus is very tender. Turn the slow cooker to high and add the boiling water and the pasta. Stir well and cook for 30 to 35 minutes, stirring a couple of times. If the liquid is all absorbed before the pasta has cooked through, add some more hot water ¼ cup (60 ml) at a time.

At the end of cooking time, remove and discard the bay leaf, then add ¼ cup (60 ml) of cold water to halt the cooking process. The pasta should be cooked through but it should also be fairly "sloppy." It will thicken more as it stands, so serve immediately. If desired, sprinkle with some grated mizithra.

Notes: Tomato passata is a medium-thick juice made of crushed and strained raw tomatoes. You should be able to find it in local stores or Greek markets, or online. You could also use a tomato puree in place of the passata, though results may vary due to some differences in water content and volume.

Depending on the brand, or where you buy your octopus, it may need cleaning before cooking. This might involve cutting out what is known as the beak. Search the Internet for videos using the phrase "how to clean an octopus" before you start.

Shrimp in Tomato and Feta Sauce

SERVES 4–6

(GARIDES SAGANAKI)

"Summer in a dish" could be a good tagline for this delicious appetizer. Think small wooden tables with rickety chairs on a little beach, white paper tablecloths and cold beer, sandy feet in flip-flops. If you've been to Greece on holiday you probably have the same picture in mind as I do. A platter of *garides saganaki* is probably on that same table, together with the tzatziki and Greek salad.

Well, here I am to tell you that you can make this dish at home in your slow cooker. It would make a great side at a garden barbecue, or an impressive appetizer at a summer dinner party. Serve with bread for dipping in the sauce, and let your guests know that using fingers to clean the shrimp is totally acceptable!

1 (14-oz [411-g]) can diced tomatoes, no salt added, with liquid

1 cup (240 ml) tomato passata (see Notes)

3 tbsp (45 ml) olive oil

1 bay leaf

1 tsp mild garlic paste

1 tsp sugar

¼ tsp chili flakes

¼ cup (60 ml) ouzo (see Notes)

1 lb (450 g) raw Pacific white shrimp, deveined with heads removed, tail and shell on (see Notes)

2 cups (255 g) feta cheese, crumbled into ½- to 1-inch (1.3- to 2.5-cm) pieces

Chopped parsley, to garnish

Crusty bread, to serve

Place the tomatoes, passata, olive oil, bay leaf, garlic paste, sugar and chili flakes into the slow cooker. Stir and cook on high for 2 to 3 hours or until the sauce is thickened.

Pour in the ouzo, stir again and lay the shrimp on top. Crumble in the feta, leaving it in fairly large pieces (they will melt slightly). Make sure you can still see some of the shrimp so you can check its color. Continue cooking on high for another 15 to 20 minutes or until the shrimp is just cooked through (it will have turned a whitish pink). Don't overcook!

Remove the bay leaf and discard. Transfer the shrimp to a platter and sprinkle with the parsley. Serve as a mezze or appetizer with lots of crusty bread.

Tip: If you have leftovers, shell the shrimp and toss it all with cooked pasta for a quick and delicious dinner.

Notes: Tomato passata is a medium-thick juice made of crushed and strained raw tomatoes. You should be able to find it in local stores or Greek markets, or online. You could also use a tomato puree in place of the passata, though results may vary due to some difference in water content and volume.

Ouzo is a dry anise-flavored aperitif, which is often diluted with water or ice. If you can't find it, you could use its sweeter cousin, Sambuca, but the results will differ as ouzo has a stronger taste.

Be sure to use raw shrimp, not pre-cooked. The color should be a translucent gray, not white or pink. They are easy to find prepared, and often available frozen as well (thaw before using).

Melt in Your Mouth Octopus and Shallot Stew

(HTAPODI STIFADO)

Like the original rabbit *stifado* (see Rabbit and Shallot Stew [Kouneli Stifado] on page 23), octopus stifado also features shallots. A whole bunch of them. It wouldn't be stifado if it didn't! The most common octopus versions use mainly wine, vinegar, tomatoes, bay leaves and allspice. I wanted to switch things up a bit since tomato and wine are the stars of the other classic octopus dish in this book, so I left these out and used balsamic vinegar, which I love. Honey is always a good idea with balsamic and not uncommon in octopus stifado, so I added some for a little sweetness. The orange zest is an unusual twist for this dish, giving a delicate but interesting flavor to the sauce.

¼ cup (60 ml) olive oil, divided

3 lb (1.4 kg) shallots, peeled (see Notes)

2 lb (900 g) octopus, bought frozen and fully defrosted, cut into large chunks if desired

5 tbsp (75 ml) balsamic vinegar

¼ cup (60 ml) honey, divided

1 tsp orange zest

1 tsp dried rosemary

½ tsp black pepper

½ tsp cinnamon

¼ tsp allspice

⅛ tsp salt

Fresh bread, to serve

Heat 2 tablespoons (30 ml) of the olive oil in a large nonstick frying pan over medium-low heat. Add the whole shallots and cook gently for 15 minutes, or until they turn a nice golden color with some spots of brown. Transfer the shallots to the slow cooker along with any oil left in the pan.

Put the octopus in the frying pan and turn the heat to high so it releases its juices. When the juices have almost all evaporated, usually after about 10 minutes, add the balsamic vinegar. Let it bubble for 30 seconds, stir in 3 tablespoons (45 ml) of honey and, as soon as it melts, tip everything into the slow cooker.

Add the orange zest, rosemary, pepper, cinnamon, allspice and salt as well as the remaining 2 tablespoons (30 ml) of olive oil. Cook on low for 5 to 7 hours, or until the octopus is very tender. Try the sauce and add the remaining tablespoon (15 ml) of honey if necessary. If there is a lot of runny sauce, prop the lid open, turn to high and continue cooking for another 30 minutes to 1 hour, until the liquid has thickened a little. It won't thicken a lot due to the quantity of water the octopus and shallots will release.

Serve with lots of fresh bread to mop up the sauce.

Notes: The trick to keeping the shallots whole while cooking is to barely "shave" the base of each shallot (where the roots are) with a sharp knife, rather that cut it off completely when peeling. This way the layers will stay attached to the base and the shallots will remain whole.

This recipe uses frozen octopus (the freezing process tenderizes it). You can try it with fresh, but keep in mind you might have to cook it for longer to get it tender. Make sure the octopus has been cleaned of its beak (see the Notes on page 73).

Fish Cooked with Tomato, Parsley and Capers

(PSARI SPETSIOTA)

One of the most popular ways to cook fish at home in Greece is *a la Spetsiota*. Similar recipes are also called *Plaki*, and like all classic dishes, both have many variations. All versions, however, seem to agree on certain ingredients, namely tomato and parsley. The fish can either be whole or filleted, so here I chose perch, which is my favorite fillet. Mild tasting, meaty and almost boneless, it never disappoints. Finally, a special mention must be made of the capers in this recipe. Although not always used in Spetsiota, I personally believe they "make" the dish, as they impart lots of flavor that complements the fish beautifully.

6 tbsp (90 ml) olive oil, divided

3 tbsp (45 ml) tomato paste

1 tsp garlic paste

1 tsp dried oregano

½ tsp sugar

½ tsp lemon pepper

¾ tsp salt

1 lb (450 g) plum tomatoes (see Notes)

2 tsp (2 g) dried onion flakes, divided

⅓ cup (20 g) parsley, finely chopped, tightly packed, divided

2 lb (900 g) white fish fillet (perch), fully thawed if frozen (see Notes)

6 tbsp (60 g) capers, rinsed from their brine and patted dry, divided

Crusty bread, to serve

In a small bowl, combine 4 tablespoons (60 ml) of olive oil, the tomato paste, garlic paste, oregano, sugar, lemon pepper and salt. Whisk with a fork to incorporate and set the sauce aside.

Slice the tomatoes into rounds of approximately ⅓-inch (8-mm) thickness and lay half of them over the bottom of the slow cooker insert.

Sprinkle the tomatoes with 1 teaspoon of onion flakes and half the parsley. Lay half the fish fillets (choose the thicker/larger ones here) on the parsley in one layer, then spread half the sauce on them. Scatter half the capers on top.

Repeat the layers starting with the rest of the tomato slices, then the onion flakes, parsley, fish, sauce and capers. Drizzle with the 2 remaining tablespoons (30 ml) of olive oil.

Cook on high for 1 to 2 hours, or until the largest fillet in the top layer flakes easily with a fork. Start keeping an eye on the fish early on and check often, because you don't want it to overcook and become rubbery.

When ready, tip the slow cooker to the side, scoop up some of the juice and spoon it over the top of the fillets. Let the fillets rest for 10 minutes before removing with a slotted spoon. Lay tomato slices and some capers on top of each piece of fish. Serve with some extra juice from the pot if desired, and lots of crusty bread.

Notes: Keep in mind that it is important for this dish to use plum tomatoes as they contain less water.

Perch in Greece is Nile perch. Check online for suppliers or closest alternatives if it's hard to find.

Whole Fish Cooked in Parchment with Lemon–Olive Oil Dressing

(PSARI LADOLEMONO)

Cooking whole fish at home might sound a little intimidating if you aren't used to it. For me, the absolute best way to prepare it without any fuss and without worrying about the result is to cook it in the slow cooker in a pouch. The foil and parchment keep the steam from escaping and ensure a moist, tender result. The fish is beautifully simple and delicate in flavor, without anything to interfere and overpower it—just as Greeks like it. The dressing, which adds a vibrant zing, is inspired by the plain *ladolemono* (oil and lemon) sauce served in Greece alongside grilled fish.

4 (12 x 15-inch [30 x 37-cm]) squares of parchment paper

4 (12 x 15-inch [30 x 37-cm]) squares of aluminum foil

4 (1-lb [454-g]) whole fish, such as orata, cleaned, heads and tails on (see Note)

4 tsp (20 ml) olive oil, divided

5 tbsp (40 g) spring onions, bulbs and tops removed, thinly sliced, divided

1 tsp peppercorns, mixed colors, divided

¼ tsp salt, divided

1 tsp dried rosemary, divided

For the dressing

¼ cup (60 ml) olive oil

¼ cup (60 ml) freshly squeezed lemon juice

1 tbsp (15 ml) Dijon mustard

1 tbsp (4 g) parsley, finely chopped, tightly packed

¼ tsp rosemary, dried

¼ tsp garlic paste

¼ tsp salt

Lay each piece of parchment paper on top of each piece of foil. Put a fish on each of the four squares. Brush each side of each fish with about ½ teaspoon of the olive oil (total 4 teaspoons [20 ml]). Sprinkle each fish or cavity with equal amounts of the spring onions, peppercorns, salt and rosemary. Bring the sides of the squares up, fold over loosely and seal the edges.

Place the foil pouches in the slow cooker in two layers (2 fish top, 2 fish bottom). It's okay if they are slightly bent. You don't need to add anything else, such as water, to the pot. Cook on high for 1 hour, then switch the order of the pouches, bringing the bottom ones to the top, and continue cooking for 50 minutes to an hour longer. (Switching the pouches is easier than it sounds as you can actually lift them with your fingers; the foil isn't too hot to handle.)

Take care not to overcook the fish or it will dry out and become rubbery.

To make the dressing, blend the olive oil, lemon juice, mustard, parsley, rosemary, garlic paste and salt in a food processor or blender until smooth.

Remove the fish from their pouches and serve with a generous drizzle of dressing. This dish goes well with potato salad, a green leafy salad or grilled summer vegetables.

Note: My favorite fish to try here is orata (also known as dorade or gilthead sea bream), freshwater trout or even red porgy (although you would have to find fairly small ones for this method). Another possibility is branzino (European bass). Ideally, you want fleshy white fish without many bones. Talk to your local fishmonger and if you can't find these types of fish, get some suggestions for alternatives.

Fresh Sardines with Cherry Tomatoes and Oregano

(SARDELES ME NTOMATINIA)

Sardines are great little fish. Very nutritious, tasty and inexpensive. In Greece you can find them canned, of course, but they are also extremely popular cooked fresh. In restaurants they are served grilled, but at home a favorite way to prepare them is to bake them in the oven with tomato.

The idea for this recipe came after my friend Eirini made something similar in her slow cooker when she moved to Scotland. Sardines there are quite a bit larger than Greek sardines, so she stuffed hers with cherry tomatoes rather than layering them, but the main idea is the same.

So, this is my take on slow cooker sardines with tomatoes. Since I often had sardines on toast as a child, I decided to combine the two and serve them bruschetta-style. And a little tip I have to share: Interestingly, when eaten with bread, you can hardly feel the tiny sardine bones that some people find annoying!

---

1 lb (450 g) cherry tomatoes, halved

¼ tsp salt, divided

¼ tsp freshly ground black pepper, divided

¾ tsp dried oregano, divided

14 oz (400 g) fresh small sardines, cleaned and filleted

2 large cloves garlic, halved or thinly sliced

3 tbsp (45 ml) olive oil

1 tsp red wine vinegar, plus extra, to serve

Sourdough bread or whole-wheat baguette, sliced and toasted

Lay about three-quarters of the tomatoes on the bottom of the slow cooker in an even layer. Sprinkle with ⅛ teaspoon of salt, ⅛ teaspoon of pepper and ¼ teaspoon of oregano.

Layer the sardines over the tomatoes so that they are overlapping, like roof tiles. Top with the rest of the tomatoes and nestle the garlic pieces among them. The halved cloves can be taken out after cooking, whereas the sliced ones stay in, so choose depending on how much you like garlic!

Sprinkle in the rest of the salt, pepper and oregano, and drizzle in the olive oil and vinegar.

Cook on high for 1 to 1½ hours, or until the sardines are cooked through. Be very watchful as they can dry out quickly.

Serve bruschetta-style on the sourdough or whole-wheat bread. Drizzle with extra vinegar if desired.

Notes: For a light meal rather than an appetizer, toast some regular sliced bread and top with the sardines and tomatoes. Allow for 2 slices per person.

Greek sardines are the species known as the European pilchard.

Calamari with Spinach and Fresh Herbs

(KALAMARIA ME SPANAKI)

The words "calamari" and "Greece" in the same sentence usually brings to mind the fried kind, am I right? The kind served in taverns alongside grilled octopus and Greek salad. Well, statistically speaking, I'm sure most calamari are indeed eaten this way in Greece. However, there are some exceptions, which are usually saved for home cooking and will rarely feature on the menu of your average seaside restaurant.

One of the exceptions is this dish, and although it's usually made with cuttlefish, variations with calamari are not uncommon. The main difference between my version and the traditional recipe is bulgur wheat. When I first tested the dish in the slow cooker I stayed as close to the original as possible. I was very pleased with it, but there was too much delicious-tasting juice from all the spinach, which I could not bring myself to discard. The bulgur wheat solved this problem, soaking up most of the juice while at the same time making the dish more substantial and filling. So, while less bread is needed, some bread is still, of course, advisable. You must know that by now!

½ cup (85 g) finely chopped onion, very tightly packed

⅔ cup (85 g) finely chopped spring onions (green parts included), tightly packed

¾ cup (40 g) dill leaves, finely chopped, lightly packed

1½ lb (680 g) mature spinach leaves (not baby spinach)

21 oz (600 g) calamari rings, bought frozen and fully defrosted, rinsed and drained well (not the breaded type)

3 tbsp (45 ml) tomato paste

2 tbsp (30 ml) mild garlic paste

½ cup (120 ml) white wine

¼ cup (60 ml) freshly squeezed lemon juice, plus extra, to serve

½ tsp sugar

¼ tsp black pepper

½ tsp chili flakes

6 tbsp (90 ml) olive oil

¼ cup (60 g) bulgur wheat (cracked wheat)

Crusty bread, to serve

Layer the onion, spring onions, dill and spinach in the slow cooker insert, in the order mentioned. Place the calamari on top.

Mix the tomato and garlic pastes into the white wine and pour over the contents of the slow cooker. Pour in the lemon juice and sprinkle with the sugar, black pepper and chili flakes. Drizzle with the olive oil.

Cook on high for 1½ to 2 hours, or until the spinach is fully wilted and there is lots of juice in the slow cooker. Add the bulgur wheat and continue cooking for another ½ to 1 hour, or until the wheat is tender (this will depend on its type and how coarsely cracked it is).

Much of the liquid will now be absorbed, but the final dish should still be very juicy. Serve with extra lemon juice if desired, and a little crusty bread for dipping.

Stuffed Lettuce Rolls with Cod and Bulgur

(MAROULODOLMADES)

SERVES 4—6

Greek cuisine has several dishes with stuffed leaves of some sort or another. Lettuce is probably the least common, which makes sense seeing as it is a little time consuming and fussy. Blanching lettuce leaves and separating them is something that needs a bit of focus and lots of patience. Nigella Lawson once said that for her, making risotto is a procedure that feels almost meditative. For me, it's this. Save this recipe for a day when you have extra time and feel like getting lost in your thoughts.

25–35 large Romaine lettuce leaves, plus extra in case some get torn

12 oz (340 g) cod, defrosted if frozen (weight thawed), very finely chopped

¼ cup (60 g) bulgur wheat

⅓ cup (60 g) minced onion, lightly packed

¼ cup (15 g) dill leaves, finely chopped, tightly packed

¼ cup (15 g) parsley leaves, finely chopped, tightly packed

2 tsp (5 g) freshly grated lemon zest

5 tbsp (75 ml) olive oil, divided

1 tbsp (15 ml) soy sauce

¼ tsp lemon pepper

1 cup (240 ml) tomato passata (see Note)

1 cup (240 ml) water

½ tsp salt

½ tsp sugar

½ tsp paprika

Fresh crusty bread, to serve

Remove the torn, outer leaves of the lettuce and discard. Separate the larger leaves and cut about 1 to 1½ inches (2.5 to 4 cm) off the tougher bottom parts of the stems.

Carefully blanch the lettuce leaves in boiling water, 4 to 5 leaves at a time, until just softened, about 2 minutes. If your lettuce is quite tough you could do more at a time. Remove with a large slotted spoon and gently set aside in a colander to cool slightly. Gently separate the leaves, starting with the first cooled ones, and lay them out on a clean surface.

Prepare the stuffing mix by combining the cod, wheat, onion, dill, parsley, lemon zest and 3 tablespoons (45 ml) of the olive oil in a large bowl. Add the soy sauce and lemon pepper, and mix well with your hands for at least 5 minutes.

Bring the stuffing close and clear some space in front of you. Take a lettuce leaf and lay it flat with the stem facing toward you. The inside of the leaf should be facing up. Put 2 or 3 tablespoons of stuffing, depending on the size of the leaf, at the base of the leaf, then bring the bottom up over the filling, fold the sides in and roll up toward the top of the leaf. Place the roll, seam side down, in the slow cooker insert. Continue with the rest of the lettuce leaves until the stuffing is gone, placing the rolls snugly beside each other. You should get about 25 to 35 rolls in two layers, depending on the size of the lettuce leaves and the amount of stuffing you use for each one. It is a good idea for all the rolls to be facing the same way for easier removal after cooking.

Stir the passata into the water and add the salt, sugar and paprika. Very gently and slowly pour the mixture over the rolls (it won't cover them). Drizzle with the remaining 2 tablespoons (30 ml) of olive oil. Place a small plate directly on top of the rolls to keep them snug and in place.

Cook on low for 2½ to 3½ hours, or until the wheat inside the rolls has softened. Turn the cooker off, spoon some sauce over the top layer of rolls and let them cool a little before removing from the insert.

Serve with crusty bread.

Note: Tomato passata is a medium-thick juice made of crushed and strained raw tomatoes. You should be able to find it in local stores or Greek markets, or online. You could also use a tomato puree in place of the passata, with varying results.

EFFORTLESS,
FLAVORFUL VEGGIES

GREEKS ARE BIG MEAT EATERS—we've already established that. However, Greek cuisine also has a multitude of classic vegetarian and vegan dishes. One of the reasons for this is the many years of poverty suffered by this war-stricken country. Poverty leads people to turn to the land in order to find sustenance and nutrition. The other reason is related to religion.

The Greek Orthodox Church observes many different fasting periods. The main one is Lent, the 40 days before Easter, but in total there are between 180 and 200 days of fasting. That is half the year! During these periods, no products originating from animals are supposed to be consumed at any time. This includes, of course, meat, fish, eggs and dairy, but does not include seafood and honey, which are allowed. Younger generations don't fast as strictly anymore, but many still do during Holy Week. Coming up with a variety of meals during a fasting period is no mean feat, which would go some way to explaining the plethora of traditional vegetarian dishes in this meat-loving country.

One of the characteristics of Greece's veggie food scene is that it's heavily seasonal, making it quite hard to find certain fruits and vegetables all year round. If you do find something that is out of season, it is usually quite expensive. Thus, many Greek dishes tend to belong exclusively to a specific time of year. For example, you wouldn't dream of making stuffed tomatoes in winter. Similarly, you won't easily find cauliflower on any menu in July. There are some exceptions of course, such as green beans and peas. These are time consuming to prepare if fresh, so the frozen varieties are very popular. Hence, they have become more or less year-round dishes. Gosh, my Greek grandmother wouldn't be happy with me saying that!

Finally, there is one fairly important thing you should know about cooking vegetables in Greece. They are usually cooked very, very well—as in, cooked until they are falling apart. Don't be surprised at the cooking times for some of these recipes, and don't be tempted to cut them short—they just won't be the same!

I hope you enjoy this section of the book; it's one of my favorites!

Famous Stuffed Tomatoes and Bell Peppers

(GEMISTA)

SERVES 4

A pretty famous dish and a personal favorite of mine, *Gemista* is a hugely popular summer food in Greece. It ignites many heated conversations about whether or not it should have meat in the stuffing (it shouldn't!) and sometimes you'll hear people arguing over whether you should eat the veggie "lids." We love to argue here, so that is totally normal. What is definitely abnormal, though, is not liking Gemista in the first place. Although usually made in the oven, they also work brilliantly in the slow cooker. As a quick reminder, these quantities are for a 6.5- or 7-quart (5.7- to 6.5-L) slow cooker.

For the potatoes

1⅓ lb (600 g) peeled potatoes, sliced into ½-inch (1-cm) rounds

½ tsp salt

¼ tsp sweet paprika

2 cloves garlic, quartered

2 tsp (10 ml) olive oil

¼–½ cup (60–120 ml) water (enough to almost cover the potatoes)

For the tomatoes and peppers

4 to 5 medium green bell peppers

4 to 5 medium tomatoes

8-10 pinches of sugar

¾ cup (155 g) long-grain rice

¼ cup (30 g) finely chopped spring onion, tightly packed

¼ cup (15 g) fresh dill leaves, finely chopped, tightly packed

¼ cup (15 g) parsley leaves, finely chopped, tightly packed

1½ tsp (3 g) sweet paprika

1 tsp salt

½ tsp minced garlic

¼ tsp black pepper

¼ cup (60 ml) olive oil, divided

Feta cheese, to serve

Crusty bread, to serve

Greek yogurt, to serve, optional

Layer the potatoes inside the slow cooker insert; try to place each slice on top of a gap in the layer below. Sprinkle with the salt and paprika. Nestle the garlic pieces among the slices and drizzle with the olive oil. Add the water.

Prepare the vegetables for stuffing, starting with the bell peppers. Slice the tops off just below the stems and keep them with the corresponding bell peppers for later use. Remove the seeds and membranes from the bell peppers carefully, then add a pinch of sugar to each and set aside.

Using a sharp, pointy knife, cut a wide circle around the stem of the tomatoes, pushing the knife in diagonally to cut under the stem. You want to cut a "lid" off each tomato, in order to remove the insides. Pull the lid up and off, and scoop the flesh and seeds out with a melon baller or a teaspoon, making sure the "walls" of the tomatoes are still fairly thick and the base isn't torn or cut. Reserve the tomato flesh, juice and seeds, and add a pinch of sugar to each tomato shell. Again, keep the lids.

Transfer the tomato flesh, juice and seeds to a bowl. Pulse two or three times for a few seconds with a stick blender to chop the flesh and create a bit more juice. Mix in the rice, spring onion, dill, parsley, paprika, salt, minced garlic, black pepper and 2 tablespoons (30 ml) of the olive oil. Fill the tomatoes and bell peppers with the mixture, reaching just over three-quarters of the way up. Put the lids back on the vegetables.

Stand the vegetables on the potatoes in the pot, so that they sit snugly next to each other. Drizzle with the remaining 2 tablespoons (30 ml) of olive oil. Cook on low for 4 to 6 hours, or until the vegetables are soft and the rice inside is fully cooked.

Let the vegetables cool slightly with the lid off before removing carefully. It might be a good idea to use your fingers for this. Serve lukewarm or at room temperature with feta cheese and crusty bread. You can also try them with Greek yogurt; it suits them, even though it's not such a common combination here in Greece.

No-Crust Spinach and Feta "Lazy" Pie

SERVES 4—6

(SPANAKOPITA XORIS FYLLO)

Pies are a huge part of Greek cuisine. There are hundreds of varieties, with pastry or without. Pastry might not work in the slow cooker, but there are other types of delicious Greek pies that do. "Lazy" pies have been given this name because they are much quicker to prepare and don't require rolling out sheets of phyllo. One could say that nowadays with store-bought pastry, all pies could be named lazy pies, but in fact, even store-bought phyllo needs a bit of effort to layer and grease each sheet. Real lazy pies have only flour and a handful more ingredients, usually including yogurt and cheese.

Here I chose to re-create the famous spanakopita (spinach pie) so there are slightly more ingredients involved. All of them, however, are easy to find and come together brilliantly in the slow cooker to create the perfect lunch box snack or light meal.

⅔ cup (85 g) all-purpose flour, lightly packed

¾ cup (110 g) cornmeal, lightly packed

½ tsp baking powder

¼ tsp freshly ground black pepper

3 eggs

1 cup plus 2 tbsp (310 g) Greek yogurt

7 tbsp (105 ml) olive oil

10 oz (310 g) baby spinach, roughly chopped

¼ cup (30 g) spring onion, finely chopped (white and light green part only), tightly packed

¼ cup (15 g) dill, finely chopped (leaves only), tightly packed

2 cups (255 g) feta cheese, crumbled into ½–1-inch (1-3-cm) pieces

In a medium-sized bowl, whisk the flour, cornmeal, baking powder and black pepper.

In a separate, large bowl whisk the eggs, yogurt and olive oil. Whisk the dry ingredients into the wet.

Stir the baby spinach, spring onion and dill into the mixture until combined. This may take some patience and elbow grease to begin with, but it will come together soon. Gently fold in the feta, trying not to crush it.

Line the slow cooker with a sling (see step-by-step instructions on page 11). Pour the batter into the insert, smooth out the surface and place a long piece of paper towel across the top of the pot, securing it in place with the lid. The paper should not touch the batter; it should sit tautly under the lid. Cook on high for 3 to 4 hours, or until the surface is set and a knife inserted in the center comes out clean.

Let the pie cool and rest in the slow cooker, without the lid, for at least a couple of hours. Then carefully pull the pie out using the sling "handles" (as shown).

Cut into slices and serve with a tomato salad.

Notes: This recipe is best served a few hours after cooking, or even the next day, after the flavors have had time to meld. It can be enjoyed warm, gently reheated in a pan or microwave, or cold.

The salt content depends very much on the type of feta used. If the feta is not very salty, you might consider adding ¼ teaspoon salt to the mixture at the same time as the black pepper.

Greek Summer Ratatouille

(BRIAM)

Another beloved summer dish for Greek people. *Briam* is delicious, uses lots of healthy summer produce and can be thrown together in the time needed to wash and cut up some veggies. It's usually cooked in the oven but also works superbly in the slow cooker. You may not get the crispiness that a hot oven gives Briam, but what you do get is the true flavor of the vegetables, which shines through with the extended low-heat cooking and can be otherwise lost. For this reason, it's worth getting great quality, organic vegetables. It makes a big difference.

The amount of olive oil might seem excessive here, but it's not. It is vital to the success of Briam. Don't skimp on it, and please use the good stuff!

1¼ lb (510 g) baby potatoes, scrubbed

2½ cups (310 g) sliced carrots

4 cups (510 g) zucchini, sliced to 1-inch (2.5-cm) thickness

1 medium onion, quartered

2 plum tomatoes, quartered

1 tbsp (3 g) finely chopped fresh dill leaves, optional

1½ tsp (9 g) coarse salt

1 tsp dried oregano

5 tbsp (75 ml) good quality olive oil

1 tbsp (15 ml) tomato paste

½ cup (120 ml) hot water

Fresh crusty bread, to serve

Feta cheese, to serve

Put the potatoes in the bottom of the slow cooker, halving any large ones. Add the carrots, zucchini, onion and tomatoes. Don't mix.

Sprinkle the dill, salt and oregano over the vegetables. Pour the olive oil over the top. Mix the tomato paste into the hot water until dissolved and pour it over the veggies. Again, don't mix the ingredients.

Cook on low for about 7 to 9 hours, or until the potatoes are soft and have taken on a reddish hue. Your veggies might seem fully cooked earlier, but it's important to leave them until they sort of caramelize and become nice and shiny and dark in color. There won't be much liquid in the pot at the beginning of the cook time, so only stir after the first few hours (if you want to) and then again toward the end of cooking.

Serve with lots of fresh crusty bread and feta cheese. Briam is also nice with Greek yogurt.

Tender Lemon–Olive Oil Peas

(ARAKAS LEMONATOS)

Peas may be considered a side dish in many cuisines, or used to bulk up other foods, like rice or pasta, but here they are the star of their own show. Plain boiled peas as a garnish would probably be left untouched by a Greek, and I'm sorry to say, if you see them mixed with rice on your plate in a Greek restaurant, it could be a good indication that you've found yourself in a somewhat touristy establishment.

Greeks prefer their peas (*Arakas*) cooked until they're falling apart, in a tomato or lemon sauce heavy on the olive oil. It's a dish with a strong homey feel to it. This lemon version (*Lemonatos*) is my favorite. Potatoes make it a little more filling, although the obscene amount of bread used to mop up the sauce can usually take care of that. Feta in this case is not optional!

2 lb (900 g) potatoes, peeled and cut into medium-sized pieces

¾ cup (110 g) finely chopped onion, lightly packed

6 tbsp (90 ml) olive oil, divided

2 lb (900 g) frozen peas, defrosted

½ cup (30 g) fresh dill, finely chopped, tightly packed

¼ cup (60 ml) freshly squeezed lemon juice

1½ tsp (9 g) salt

½ tsp black pepper

1½ cups (360 ml) vegetable stock

Feta cheese and crusty bread, to serve

Combine the potatoes, onions and 3 tablespoons (45 ml) of the olive oil in the bottom of the slow cooker. Layer the peas on top, then the dill. Don't stir from now on, so as not to disturb the layers.

Stir the lemon juice, salt and pepper into the vegetable stock and pour it over the ingredients in the slow cooker pot. Drizzle the rest of the olive oil on top and cook on low for 6 to 8 hours.

The dish is ready when the peas and potatoes are very soft and starting to fall apart. The peas should be a dark green color as opposed to the vibrant green they are when raw. If you can, wait for about 15 minutes before serving.

Serve with crusty bread and feta cheese.

Artichokes with Potatoes and Carrots in Egg-Lemon Sauce

(AGGINARES AVGOLEMONO)

Artichokes in egg-lemon are a popular variation of a classic dish called artichokes *a la Polita*. The original a la Polita was developed by the Greek chef Nikolaos Tselementes in the early twentieth century and was based on a recipe from Constantinople (now Istanbul) in Turkey. The original version was a simple artichoke, shallot and olive oil stew, with the chef adapting it to include potatoes and carrots. It is widely enjoyed this way today, but many (myself included) like to add an egg-lemon sauce. Personally, I add egg-lemon sauce to absolutely anything I possibly can.

Having written the first contemporary Greek cookbook in 1910, Tselementes is considered to be one of the most important figures in our cuisine's history. With his vast experience working in French, Italian and U.S. restaurants, he single-handedly modernized Greek cooking and brought previously unheard-of methods and recipes to the average Greek household (a good example is béchamel sauce, which today features in many dishes like moussaka). His books were so popular that in Greek the name "Tselementes" is actually synonymous with "cookbook." Although this seemed like a good thing at the time, many of today's experts consider his influence on traditional Greek food to be equal to vandalism.

And with that tidbit of unrelated trivia, let's have a look at these artichokes.

---

1 lb (450 g) peeled potatoes, cut into 1–1½-inch (2.5–4-cm) pieces

1⅓ cups (170 g) sliced carrots

1⅓ cups (140 g) finely chopped spring onions, lightly packed

2 lb (900 g) frozen artichoke bottoms

¼ cup (15 g) dill, finely chopped, tightly packed

1½ cups (360 ml) warm vegetable stock

¼ cup plus 2 tbsp (90 ml) freshly squeezed lemon juice, divided

1½ tsp (9 g) salt

¾ tsp black pepper

3 tbsp (45 ml) olive oil

2 eggs

Feta cheese and crusty bread, to serve

Place potatoes, carrots and onions in the slow cooker insert, stir, add the frozen artichokes on top and sprinkle with the dill. Don't stir from now on.

Combine the stock, 2 tablespoons (30 ml) of the lemon juice, salt and pepper and pour the mixture over the artichokes. Drizzle with the olive oil.

Cook on low for 5 to 7 hours, or until the potatoes and carrots are cooked through.

Beat the eggs in a large bowl and slowly add ¼ cup (60 ml) of the lemon juice, continuing to beat the mixture as you add.

Turn the slow cooker off and bring the bowl close to your slow cooker. Carefully temper the egg mixture by taking one spoonful of hot liquid at a time from the insert and adding it to the bowl while whisking continuously. Do this patiently so the mixture in the bowl warms up slowly without the eggs scrambling. Start with small amounts, 1 tablespoon (15 ml) at first, and increase the amount as you go up to ½ cup (120 ml). When most of the cooking liquid has been added to the egg mixture and the bowl is hot to the touch, pour the sauce back into the slow cooker. Holding the slow cooker by the side handles, move it gently in circular motions so the sauce is distributed evenly.

Let the vegetables rest in the slow cooker with the lid on for a few minutes before serving. Enjoy with feta cheese and lots of crusty bread to mop up the sauce.

Stuffed Vine Leaves with Rice

(DOLMADAKIA)

SERVES 6—8

You are probably familiar with the term *dolma*. The origin of the word is thought to come from the Turkish word *dolmak* (to fill). Stuffed vegetables of all kinds, however, feature in many cuisines, from Middle Eastern all the way to Italian.

In Greece, the specific word *dolmadakia* means stuffed vine leaves (grape leaves) with rice, herbs and in some cases ground meat. Depending on the area, they might range from small to tiny. Tiny "packages" that deliver a burst of flavor when popped in your mouth!

Here I'm sharing my favorite, the rice version. It's amazing how a few simple ingredients can deliver such a delicious result. These dolmadakia are best enjoyed at room temperature with Greek yogurt.

For the filling

6 tbsp (90 ml) olive oil, divided

¾ cup (110 g) finely chopped onion, lightly packed

1 cup (110 g) finely chopped spring onions, lightly packed

1 cup (200 g) long-grain rice uncooked

¾ cup plus 1 tbsp (195 ml) water

½ cup (30 g) finely chopped dill leaves, tightly packed

½ cup (30 g) finely chopped parsley leaves, tightly packed

¼ cup (15 g) finely chopped spearmint leaves, tightly packed

¾ tsp salt

¼ tsp black pepper

For the dolmadakia

40-50 vine leaves, plus 4-5 extra, preserved in brine, carefully separated, rinsed and drained, stalks removed

¼ tsp salt, divided

¼ tsp black pepper, divided

To make the filling, place 4 tablespoons (60 ml) of the olive oil, the onions and the spring onions in a large, nonstick frying pan over medium heat (no need to heat the oil first). Let the onions cook for 10 minutes, or until softened. Add the rice, stir to coat and cook for 3 minutes, stirring continuously. Add the water, stir and cook for 3 to 5 minutes, until the water has been absorbed and the mixture is dry.

Take the pan off the heat and add the remaining 2 tablespoons (30 ml) of olive oil, dill, parsley, spearmint, salt and pepper. Stir well.

To make the dolmadakia, clear some space in front of you on a clean work surface, and bring the filling, the vine leaves and the slow cooker insert close by.

Place a prepared vine leaf on the work surface, with the side with the veins facing upwards. Take a tablespoon of the mixture, either level or rounded depending on the size of the leaf, and put it toward the bottom end of the leaf, near where the stalk was. Fold the left and right sides up and over the filling, then bring the bottom up and roll toward the top, creating a tube-shaped parcel. Place it in the slow cooker insert with the seal on the bottom. See page 102 for how to fill and roll dolmadakia.

Continue with all the vine leaves and stuffing, placing the dolmadakia close to each other snugly. There should be no spaces between any of them, or they might open up during cooking. There will be one full layer and one that may not be complete. Sprinkle about ⅛ teaspoon salt and ⅛ teaspoon pepper between each layer.

Drizzle the top layer with the 3 tablespoons (45 ml) of olive oil and the lemon juice.

Lay the extra leaves, unstuffed and open, on top of the dolmadakia to cover them. This will help to keep them moist while cooking. Place a small plate on top (it should be small enough to fit in the pot and sit on top of the dolmadakia) to keep everything in place. No need to invert it as it's easier to lift out if it's the right way up.

Pour water very gently and slowly over the dolmadakia, to the side of the plate, until it's just covering them. Cook on low for 3 to 4 hours, or until most of the water has been absorbed and the stuffed vine leaves are glossy from the oil. Turn the slow cooker off and let the dolmadakia cool completely in the insert. They will absorb the rest of the liquid while resting.

(continued)

Stuffed Vine Leaves with Rice (Continued)

3 tbsp (45 ml) olive oil, plus extra, to serve

3 tbsp (45 ml) freshly squeezed lemon juice, plus extra, to serve

Water, to cover rolls

Greek yogurt, to serve

Serve the dolmadakia at room temperature, with a drizzle of olive oil if desired, a squeeze of lemon and a dollop of Greek yogurt.

How to fill and roll dolmadakia

1.

Lay out a vine leaf, with veins facing up. Snip off the stalk of the leaf at its base.

2.

Place a tablespoon (15 g) of filling just above where the stalk was.

3.

Lift the bottom parts of the leaf over the filling.

4.

Fold the sides over towards the center.

5.

Start rolling upwards from the base . . . all the way to the top . . .

6.

. . . until you get the perfect dolmadaki!

Cabbage Rolls with Mushrooms and Tangy Lemon Dressing

(LAHANODOLMADES NISTISIMI)

Stuffed cabbage leaves, or *lahanodolmades*, are very popular here in Greece. The most common version has a meat and rice filling, similar to that of Stuffed Zucchini in Thick Egg-Lemon Sauce (Kolokythakia Gemista) on page 58. They are gorgeous that way and could, of course, be made easily in the slow cooker, but I felt that it would be more interesting to share a lesser-known version here. The word *nistisimi* means "for fasting," so as you might have guessed, these are vegan and thus suitable for Lent. This version of lahanodolmades isn't really traditional, at least to my knowledge. It came about in modern times, probably by people looking for something more exciting than the usual Lenten menu. This recipe is based on one I found in my huge box of cut-outs and handwritten recipe notes from years ago. The original was given to me by a friend and colleague after I tried her lunch at the office one day. Hara, here are your lahanodolmades, slightly messed with, but still as delicious!

Before I leave you to it, I have to mention that if there is one dish that benefits from resting overnight, it's this one. They are absolutely, certainly, positively better the next day. And don't skip the dressing—it suits the cabbage rolls perfectly.

---

1 (4½-lb [2 kg]) green cabbage

2 tsp (12 g) salt, divided

1¾ cups (170 g) coarsely grated sweet potato, lightly packed

¾ cup (110 g) finely chopped onion, lightly packed

1 cup (110 g) coarsely grated zucchini, very lightly packed

⅔ cup (140 g) grated tomatoes, skin discarded

⅔ cup (85 g) coarsely grated carrots

1 cup (85 g) finely chopped white mushrooms

¼ cup (15 g) finely chopped fresh dill, leaves and very thin stalks only, tightly packed

¼ cup (15 g) finely chopped parsley, leaves only, tightly packed

¾ cup (170 g) long-grain rice

10 tbsp (150 ml) olive oil, divided

½ tsp lemon pepper

Start by softening the cabbage leaves in preparation for stuffing. Cut out as much of the core as you can and place the whole head, cut side down, into a large saucepan of boiling water, to which you have already added 1 teaspoon of salt. Turn the heat to medium-high and let the cabbage boil for 10 to 12 minutes, flipping over after about 8 minutes. Take it out carefully with a slotted spoon and peel off the softened outer leaves. If the center is still difficult to separate, put the cabbage back in the hot water for a few minutes longer. Place all the individual leaves into a large colander. See the Note on page 105 for an alternative softening method.

Prepare the filling by combining the sweet potato, onion, zucchini, tomatoes, carrots, mushrooms, dill, parsley, rice, 6 tablespoons (90 ml) of the olive oil, 1 teaspoon salt, lemon pepper and paprika in a large bowl. Mix well with your hands.

Bring the cabbage and stuffing near. Lay a leaf out in front of you (curving upwards) and place 2 to 4 measured tablespoons of stuffing mixture (depending on the size of the leaf) at the base where the thicker part of the stem is. Bring the bottom up and over the stuffing, then fold the sides in. Roll from the bottom to the top, making sure the sides are tucked in.

If you have any large leaves with stems that are still too hard to fold over, cut them into two smaller pieces, removing the tough parts. Fill the two separate pieces as you would the others, using slightly less of the mixture if necessary.

As you prepare each roll, place it into the slow cooker insert with the seam facing down. Arrange the rolls snugly together, leaving no gaps. You should have two or three layers and 20 to 25 rolls.

(continued)

Cabbage Rolls with Mushrooms and Tangy Lemon Dressing (Continued)

1 tsp sweet paprika

¼ cup (60 ml) freshly squeezed lemon juice

2½–3⅓ cups (600-800 ml) hot vegetable stock

For the dressing

½ cup (120 ml) cooking liquid, from the slow cooker

½ cup plus 2 tbsp (150 ml) olive oil

½ cup (120 ml) freshly squeezed lemon juice

4 tsp (20 ml) prepared yellow mustard

1 tsp salt

1 tsp lemon pepper

¼ cup (15 g) finely chopped dill leaves, tightly packed

¼ cup (15 g) finely chopped parsley leaves, tightly packed

1½ cups (400 g) Greek yogurt, optional

Fresh bread, to serve

Stir 4 tablespoons (60 ml) of the olive oil and the lemon juice into the vegetable stock and pour it into the slow cooker so that it comes up to about the middle of the top layer of cabbage rolls.

Cook on low for 5 to 7 hours, or until the rolls are glossy and the rice inside is cooked through. Remove the rolls gently and transfer them to a platter to cool, reserving ½ cup (120 ml) of the cooking liquid.

To make the dressing, transfer the reserved cooking liquid to a bowl and whisk in the olive oil, lemon juice, mustard, salt, lemon pepper, dill and parsley. You can use a stick blender if desired. If you'd like a creamier, sauce-like dressing, add the Greek yogurt.

Serve the cabbage rolls lukewarm at most—room temperature or cold ideally—with the lemon dressing and some fresh bread.

Note: Another great way to soften cabbage is to freeze it before use. Just pop the whole cabbage in the freezer, leave it for a couple of days to freeze completely and then defrost it. The cabbage will have magically softened and you will be able to separate the leaves easily. But just so you know, it's still rather smelly!

Green Bean and Tomato Olive Oil Stew

(FASOLAKIA)

Out of all my recipes, I think *Fasolakia* is the one I make most often. It's the Mister's favorite and it's just so easy to throw together.

Green beans will rarely be seen on a Greek table in any other form than this: cooked with tomato and lots of olive oil, until they are fall-apart tender. If green beans have any trace of crunch left in them, they are considered undercooked. This is actually the secret to the proper preparation of the dish. When it's ready, the beans are soft, the flavor is full and the tomato is saucy but not thick. Just right for mopping up with good crusty bread. And again, you can't forget the feta. In my house, if there is no feta, we don't eat Fasolakia.

1½ lb (680 g) potatoes, peeled and cut into fairly large pieces

½ cup (85 g) finely chopped onion, very tightly packed

2 lb (900 g) green beans, bought frozen, fully defrosted

1 (28-oz [794-g]) can diced tomatoes, no salt added, with liquid

2 tsp (12 g) salt

2 tsp (4 g) sweet paprika

1 tsp sugar

Black pepper, to taste

5 tbsp (75 ml) olive oil

Feta, to serve

Crusty bread, to serve

Greek yogurt, to serve, optional

Combine the potatoes and onion in the bottom of the slow cooker. Layer the green beans on top. Don't mix from now on so the layers are not disturbed. Pour the tomatoes onto the beans.

Sprinkle in the salt, paprika, sugar and pepper. Drizzle with the olive oil and tease with a spoon so the seasoning mixes into the tomatoes.

Cook on low for 7 to 8 hours without stirring, until the vegetables are very soft and the liquid has become saucy, although it will still be runny. They may seem ready earlier, but the dish needs the extra time to come together. Give everything a good stir so the tomato is well incorporated. Let it rest for at least 15 minutes.

Serve with lots of feta and crusty bread for dipping. As with the Gemista (page 91) and the Briam (page 95) recipes, this is another dish that is lovely with a dollop of Greek yogurt. Mixed into the tomato, it creates a wonderfully creamy and slightly tangy sauce.

Super Simple and Flavorful Boiled Greens "Salad"

(HORTA)

I only discovered fairly recently that *Horta* can be made in the slow cooker. I'd never thought to try, until my friend Eirini sent me a message one day from Scotland, raving about some spinach she made in the little slow cooker I had given her. I was rather gob-smacked and very impressed at her ingenuity. I immediately wanted to try it with greens that are popular here in Greece. As it happens, the method works beautifully with beet greens, amaranth (known here as *vlita*) and chard.

Horta salad is a very simple dish, consisting of just cooked greens, good olive oil and a splash of lemon juice. Sometimes the greens are served with other boiled vegetables like zucchini. The slow cooker is a great way to cook both, with minimum mess, minimum effort and maximum flavor.

2 lb (900 g) beetroot, chard or amaranth greens with stalks, roughly chopped (in 2 or 3 pieces if large)

6 small, whole zucchinis, ends removed, optional

¼–½ tsp salt

1 cup (240 ml) water

6 tbsp (90 ml) olive oil, plus extra, to serve

Lemon juice, to serve

Crusty bread, to serve

Feta cheese, to serve

Wash the greens under the tap and shake off excess water. Don't worry too much about drying them; just shake well and transfer to the slow cooker insert while they are still wet. Push them down to fit (they will lose most of their volume during cooking so don't worry if they seem like a lot). Put the whole zucchinis on top, if using.

If using the beetroot or chard, sprinkle it with ¼ teaspoon salt; if using the amaranth, increase the amount of salt to ½ teaspoon. Pour the water over the top and drizzle in the olive oil. Cook on low for 3 to 4 hours, or until the greens are fully wilted. The stalks should be soft when squeezed between your fingers and the zucchini should be easily pierced with a sharp knife.

Remove the zucchini and then the greens with tongs, taking some of the juice with them. Discard any liquid left in the pot. Serve with an extra drizzle of olive oil if desired, a squeeze of lemon juice, crusty bread and feta cheese.

Notes   If you buy a bunch of whole beets, use the bulbs to make the "Roasted" Beet Salad Dip with Greek Yogurt and Cream (*Pantzarosalata*) on page 122. Keep in mind they will have to be cooked separately as they have different cooking times.

It is best to use small (or "baby") zucchini for this recipe to ensure that they cook in the same amount of time as the greens.

Greek "Risotto" with Leeks, Sultanas and Fresh Herbs

(PRASORYZO)

When you see a dish with a name ending in -oryzo, it means it's a rice dish. *Ryzi* is the word for rice, and here it's combined with *praso*, which means leek. So, leek-rice . . . it's kind of self-explanatory, isn't it? Here I've jazzed up the classic recipe a bit, adding some sultanas and a little grated cheese at the end. Small touches that make quite an impact. Despite me borrowing the term for the title of this recipe, rice dishes in Greek cuisine are quite different from Italian risottos and tend to be slightly firmer. Although that depends largely on personal preference, with some liking theirs "sloppier" than others. So, see how you like the texture at the end of cooking, and adjust the last step accordingly.

½ cup (60 g) finely chopped onion, lightly packed

½ cup (60 g) finely chopped spring onions, white and light green parts only, tightly packed

1¼ lb (540 g) leeks, thinly sliced, white and light green parts only

¼ cup (15 g) fresh, chopped dill leaves, tightly packed

¼ cup (15 g) fresh, chopped parsley leaves, tightly packed

1½ tsp (9 g) salt, divided

5 tbsp (75 ml) olive oil, divided

1 cup (240 ml) hot water

1 cup (200 g) uncooked long grain rice

¼ cup (40 g) sultanas, tightly packed

2 tbsp (30 ml) freshly squeezed lemon juice

2 tsp (1 g) dried spearmint

1 tsp lemon pepper

2 cups (480 ml) hot vegetable stock

½–¾ cup (120–180 ml) water, room temperature

Gruyère cheese, grated, to serve

Combine the onions, spring onions, leeks, dill, parsley and ½ teaspoon of salt in the slow cooker. Drizzle in 3 tablespoons (45 ml) of the olive oil and stir well to coat. Add the hot water.

Cook on high for 1½ to 2½ hours, or until the leeks have softened. Stir once if the leeks start scorching/burning.

Add the rice and sultanas to the slow cooker and stir them well to coat. Drizzle in the lemon juice and the remaining 2 tablespoons (30 ml) of olive oil. Sprinkle with the spearmint, remaining salt and lemon pepper, then pour in the vegetable stock.

Continue cooking on high for 1 hour if your cooker has an aluminum pot, and 1½ hours if it has a ceramic pot, or until the rice is cooked through. Turn the cooker off and add the ½ to ¾ cup (120 to 180 ml) of water to give it some moisture. Stir well. The mixture should be fairly wet since it will thicken further as it rests.

Serve the Prasoryzo with a generous sprinkling of grated Greek Gruyère cheese. Sheep or goat milk Gruyère works well here.

Crustless Zucchini "Pie" with Trahanas

(KOLOKYTHOPITA ME TRAHANA)

This pie is also known as *Tarkasi* and is a type of "lazy" pie, similar to the No-Crust Spinach and Feta "Lazy" Pie (*Spanakopita xoris Fyllo*) on page 92. The main difference in this version compared to other pies is the use of *trahanas*. Trahanas is made of flour or cracked wheat, mixed with either fresh or sour milk, dried out in the sun and broken into small, tasty clusters of grains. There are several varieties within Greece, and indeed many more in Middle Eastern and Balkan countries. (If you can't find trahanas at your local grocer or organic market, it can be found online.) It is usually cooked into a thick soup (see Creamy, Nourishing Trahana Soup [*Trahanas*] on page 153) or porridge, with stock, water or milk. It absorbs liquid very well and acts as a thickener in many recipes. Here, it helps solidify the pie.

This *Kolokythopita*, or zucchini pie, is the perfect snack; it can be enjoyed warm or cold and makes a great addition to any lunch box.

---

4 cups (510 g) zucchini, coarsely grated, very loosely packed

½ tsp salt

3 eggs

2 tbsp (30 ml) olive oil

2 tbsp (30 ml) milk

1 tsp dried spearmint

¼ tsp freshly ground black pepper,

½ cup (85 g) sour trahanas

½ cup (60 g) coarsely grated Gruyère cheese (see Note), tightly packed

1 cup (110 g) feta, crumbled into ½- to 1-inch (1.3- to 2.5-cm) pieces

Place the zucchini in a colander, sprinkle it with the salt and let it sit for about 30 minutes.

While you are waiting for the zucchini to release its water, prepare the slow cooker by making a sling (see instructions on page 11).

In a large bowl, lightly beat the eggs and whisk in the olive oil, milk, spearmint and black pepper. Stir in the trahanas and Gruyère, then gently fold in the feta.

After the zucchini has rested, squeeze it very well with your hands to remove the excess liquid. Break it up and fold it into the egg and cheese mixture.

Pour the mixture into the slow cooker and place a piece of paper towel along the top (it should not be touching the mixture, just sitting under the lid). Put the lid on and turn the cooker to high. Cook for 1½ to 2 hours, or until the surface has set. It might still be a little moist, but not runny. A cake tester or toothpick inserted into the center should come out clean. Let the pie cool slightly in the insert.

Using the two sling "handles," gently lift the pie out of the insert, slice it and serve with a leafy green or tomato salad.

Note: I recommend the Gruyère cheese from Naxos to fully complement the flavors of this dish.

Slow Cooker Greek "Roasted" Potatoes

(PATATES FOURNOU)

Roasted potatoes might seem an odd choice for a slow cooker recipe. Indeed, if you want them crispy and crunchy, this isn't the way to make them. If, however, you've tried classic Greek roasted potatoes, you'll know that they are in a league of their own. Cooked with generous amounts of olive oil, lemon juice, oregano and often water or stock, they take on a velvety soft texture that is quite special.

Here I've added a little twist that works fantastically well: sheep's milk butter! It's very popular in Greece and has a very strong, distinct flavor. I wouldn't spread it on my bread, but it works wonders in cooking. If sheep's milk butter is not your thing, just use regular cow's milk butter instead, or even extra olive oil to keep it vegan— no matter which you choose, the potatoes are sure to be delicious.

This is an ideal side dish for oven roasted, grilled or barbecued meat. Alternatively, serve the potatoes with a nice omelet or a large green salad.

3 lb (1.4 kg) large potatoes, peeled

¼ cup (60 ml) freshly squeezed lemon juice

3 tbsp (45 ml) olive oil

2 tbsp (30 g) sheep's milk butter or regular butter, melted

4 tsp (20 ml) prepared yellow mustard

2 tsp (12 g) salt

2 tsp (4 g) dried oregano

1½ tsp (3 g) dried rosemary

½ tsp lemon pepper

1 cup (240 ml) boiling water

Cut the potatoes into eighths, so that they form wedges. Put them into the slow cooker insert.

Combine the lemon juice, olive oil, butter, mustard, salt, oregano, rosemary and lemon pepper in a clean jar with a lid and shake until smooth. Pour this mixture over the potatoes and toss with your fingers to coat them well.

Pour the hot water into the slow cooker insert, pouring to the side so it doesn't rinse the oil mixture off the potatoes. Cook on low for 6 to 7 hours, or until the potatoes are cooked through and very soft.

My Go-To Simple Fresh-Tomato Sauce

(KOKKINI SALTSA)

Greece has gorgeous tomatoes, as one would expect in a country with a climate like ours. To say they are widely consumed would be the understatement of the year. Interestingly though, they only made their appearance in Greece in the early nineteenth century. In the relatively short time since then, they have managed to become one of the most important elements of Greek cooking.

Tomatoes are a summer produce and although they are available all year round, the taste and overall quality of those found in winter cannot be compared to the real thing—the tomatoes of summer. For this reason, come September, many people take to sauce-making, canning, drying, freezing and generally preserving tomatoes in any possible way.

A good tomato sauce is one of the most useful things to have in the freezer. Yes, you can find great store-bought sauces, but if you have a slow cooker, why not make a big batch to have on hand? It's easy and requires minimum effort. Here is my favorite.

6 lb (2.7 kg) ripe tomatoes

1¼ cups (170 g) finely chopped onion, lightly packed

½ cup (120 ml) olive oil

¼ cup (60 ml) tomato paste

2 tsp (4 g) dried basil

2 tsp (4 g) dried oregano

2 tsp (4 g) dried thyme

2 tsp (4 g) sweet paprika

2 tsp (8 g) sugar

1½ tsp (9 g) salt

½ tsp freshly ground black pepper

Bring a large pot of water to a boil on the stove. Make two slits in the shape of a cross on the skin at the bottom of each tomato. Pop the tomatoes in the boiling water and leave them for a minute or two, until the skins start to loosen. Lift the tomatoes out with a slotted spoon and let them cool. Do this in batches if necessary. Pinch the skins with your fingers; they should slide off easily. If they don't, pop them back into the boiling water for another minute or so.

Remove the stems and chop the tomatoes. Transfer them to the slow cooker insert.

Add the onion, olive oil, tomato paste, basil, oregano, thyme, paprika, sugar, salt and pepper to the slow cooker, stir and cook on high for 7 to 8 hours.

If the sauce has not thickened enough at this time, prop the lid open with a wooden spoon and let it cook until it reaches the desired thickness. It should take from 30 minutes to 2 hours longer, depending on the water content of the tomatoes.

Serve over pasta or freeze in portions to use in other recipes.

Note: You can omit the skinning step if you don't mind small bits of tomato skin in your sauce. It's entirely up to you.

Greek Spinach and Dill "Risotto"

(SPANAKORYZO)

Like its cousin Prasoryzo (Greek "Risotto" with Leeks, Sultanas and Herbs, page 110), this Greek spinach-rice is a wonderfully simple, tasty and healthy dish. The flavors complement each other beautifully and are made to shine with the addition of some feta cheese and extra lemon upon serving.

Spanakoryzo is another favorite in our house, and since discovering that it can be made easily in the slow cooker, it features on our menu even more frequently.

1⅓ cups (280 g) long-grain rice

1⅓ cups (140 g) finely chopped spring onions (white and green parts), lightly packed

½ cup (120 ml) olive oil, divided

6 tbsp (90 ml) freshly squeezed lemon juice, divided

1¼ cups (60 g) dill leaves, finely chopped, lightly packed, plus more to serve

2 lb (900 g) fresh large-leaf spinach, no large stalks, roughly chopped

1½ tsp (9 g) salt

1 tsp lemon pepper

3¼ cups (780 ml) hot water, plus more if needed

¼ cup (60 ml) cold water

2 tbsp (30 g) butter, optional

Feta, to serve

Bread, to serve

Combine the rice and spring onions in the slow cooker insert and drizzle with 3 tablespoons (45 ml) of the olive oil and 3 tablespoons (45 ml) of the lemon juice. Stir to coat.

Scatter the dill on top, then the spinach. Push the spinach down so it fits, little by little if necessary. It might seem impossible to begin with, but it will fit. Don't mix.

Sprinkle with the salt and lemon pepper, then drizzle with 3 tablespoons (45 ml) of the olive oil and the remaining lemon juice. Pour the 3¼ cups (780 ml) of hot water over the top.

Set the slow cooker to low and cook without stirring for about 1½ hours if your cooker has an aluminum pot, and 2 hours if it has a ceramic pot. Working swiftly so as not to leave the lid off for too long, move the spinach to the side a little, scoop some rice out and try it. If it's cooked through and no longer nutty in the center, give the whole thing a very good stir with a wooden spoon so that the spinach breaks up and mixes into the rice. If the rice is not quite cooked yet, leave it a bit longer, checking it every 15 minutes. If during this extra time all the liquid is absorbed, add ¼ cup (60 ml) of hot water. Repeat if necessary.

When ready, mix well as described above, turn the slow cooker off, and add ¼ cup (60 ml) of cold water, the butter and the remaining 2 tablespoons (30 ml) of olive oil. Stir, let it rest for 5 to 10 minutes and serve.

Keep in mind the spanakoryzo should be quite moist. Serve with extra lemon juice, feta and bread.

Note: The butter can be omitted for a vegan version of this dish.

Pasta with Fragrant Eggplant and Sweet Wine Sauce

(PSEFTOPETINOS)

Pseftopetinos was unknown to me until I started researching this book. It originates from the island of Lemnos, and the name literally means "fake rooster"! According to a famous Greek chef, it's named that way because the eggplant is supposed to be cooked whole, and the stalk looks like the comb of a rooster. A different explanation found online is that this dish is the poor man's version of rooster in tomato sauce, hence, fake/pretend rooster.

Several of the versions I found used white wine in the recipe but I decided to switch that with Mavrodafni, a dessert red originating from the Achaia region of the Peloponnese. The dark purple tones of both the wine and eggplant just made the combination feel very right. As it turns out, the sweetness of this special wine complements the sauce perfectly.

¾ cup (110 g) finely chopped onion, lightly packed

1 lb (450 g) eggplant, cut into large cubes

6 oz (170 g) roasted red peppers (preserved in brine), drained and roughly chopped

1 (28-oz [794-g]) can diced tomatoes, no salt added, with liquid

¼ cup (60 ml) Mavrodafni wine, or preferred sweet red wine

2 tbsp (30 ml) tomato paste

1½ tsp (9 g) salt

½ tsp freshly ground black pepper

1 tsp dried oregano

1 bay leaf

¼ cup (60 ml) olive oil

1 lb (450 g) uncooked fusilli, tagliatelle or pappardelle pasta

Crumbled feta cheese or grated Greek Gruyère cheese, to serve

Add the onions, eggplant, roasted red peppers, tomatoes, sweet red wine, tomato paste, salt, pepper, oregano and bay leaf to the slow cooker. Drizzle the olive oil over the top and stir gently.

Cook on high for 5 to 6 hours, or until the eggplant is soft. If the sauce is runny, prop the lid open with the handle of a wooden spoon and continue cooking until the sauce has reached the desired thickness. Remove the bay leaf and discard before serving.

When the sauce is almost ready, cook the pasta according to package instructions. Serve with a generous helping of crumbled feta or grated Gruyère.

Notes: The original Pseftopetinos is usually served with handmade pasta from Lemnos Island, called *Flomaria*, but my version works well with dried pasta too. Fusilli is a good choice but it's also delicious with long, flat pasta such as tagliatelle or pappardelle.

Mavrodafni wine is best for this dish and well worth finding online, but you can also try it with your own preferred sweet red wine.

"Roasted" Beet Salad Dip with Greek Yogurt and Cream

(PANTZAROSALATA)

Beetroot is one of my favorite vegetables. I didn't like it as a child, but when I tried it again somewhere in my twenties, I fell in love with it. As far as cooking methods go, the winner hands-down is the slow cooker. In terms of flavor and texture, it's up there with oven-roasted beetroot. But in terms of ease? It's off-the-charts better. The cherry on the cake is that it's also more wallet-friendly. I first started using this method after I discovered how easy it is to "bake" potatoes this way. Wash, rub with a little oil if desired and cook until tender. While potatoes can be eaten with their skins on, beets can be peeled within seconds once cooked, since the skins just slip off at the slightest touch. If you like beetroot, I can't recommend this method enough.

Greek beetroot salad usually has boiled beets, yogurt and walnuts in it. When I first started developing this recipe, I remembered my mum telling me some years ago about a fantastic beetroot salad she had while on holiday with my aunt on a nearby island. They both loved it and ordered it again and again. The cook at the restaurant told them the secret was to add cream. It sounded gorgeous, so I decided to try it. And gorgeous it is, indeed.

---

2 lb (900 g) whole beetroot, unpeeled

1 tsp plus 3 tbsp (50 ml) olive oil, divided

1 cup (300 g) Greek yogurt

½ cup plus 2 tbsp (150 ml) heavy cream

2 tbsp (30 ml) cider vinegar

1½ tsp (7 ml) whole-grain mustard

1½ tsp (7 ml) mild garlic paste

1½ tsp (9 g) salt

½ tsp freshly ground black pepper, or to taste

½ cup (60 g) coarsely chopped walnuts

Crusty bread or crackers, to serve

Wash the beetroot well, but don't peel it, then rub it with 1 teaspoon of the olive oil—1 teaspoon should be enough for all of it, but use a little more if necessary. Place the bulbs in the slow cooker insert without any additional ingredients; no water is necessary. Cook on low for 6 to 8 hours, or until a knife glides easily into the center of the largest one.

When the beetroot is cooked, let it cool slightly and rub each bulb to remove the skins. They should slip off easily. Cut the bulbs into small cubes and set aside.

In a large bowl, whisk the Greek yogurt, cream, vinegar, mustard, garlic paste, salt, pepper and the remaining 3 tablespoons (45 ml) of the olive oil.

Add the beetroot cubes and the walnuts, mix gently and let the salad rest for a few hours. This will help the flavors to mingle.

Serve with crusty bread or crackers. This salad also makes a lovely side dish for fish.

Comforting Tomato Soup with Orzo

(KRITHARAKI SOUPA)

This simple yet delicious soup brings back fond memories for many Greek people. A frugal dish, it used to be comprised mainly of tomato, dried pasta and meat stock for flavor and extra nutrition, since it was often made for children. The consistency would depend on personal preference, with some choosing to go for a much thicker version.

The recipe I am sharing here is slightly jazzed up, since ingredients nowadays are plentiful and a few extra components can add a lot of depth to the flavors. I've also gone for a vegetable stock rather than beef, in order to keep the dish vegetarian. Feel free to use either. The cheese on toast is also my own idea, influenced of course by my English side. And it suits the soup so well.

¾ cup (110 g) finely chopped onion, lightly packed

5 tbsp (75 ml) olive oil

6 medium-sized, ripe plum tomatoes, cut into chunks

1 tbsp (15 ml) tomato paste

1 tbsp (15 ml) balsamic vinegar

1 tbsp (15 ml) honey

1 bay leaf

1 tsp salt

½ tsp black pepper

¼ tsp allspice

4 cups (960 ml) hot vegetable stock

2 cups (480 ml) hot water

7 oz (200 g) orzo

4 large slices of bread

Coarsely grated Greek Gruyère cheese, to taste

Combine the onions and olive oil in the bottom of the slow cooker insert. Place the tomatoes on top and add the tomato paste, vinegar, honey, bay leaf, salt, pepper, allspice, vegetable stock and hot water. Cook on low for 5½ to 6½ hours.

Remove and discard the bay leaf, then use a stick blender to blitz the soup until it's smooth.

Turn the slow cooker to high, add the orzo, stir well and let it cook through. Check after 20 minutes and leave it a little longer if necessary; it could take up to 40 minutes depending on the quality and type of orzo.

While the orzo is cooking, preheat your broiler and line a baking tray with foil. Place the bread on the tray and broil until nicely browned. Remove the tray, flip the bread and top it with the cheese. Broil until the cheese is melted and bubbling.

Serve the hot soup with a slice of cheese on toast.

Tip: Greek Gruyère cheese from Naxos is an excellent choice for the toast in this recipe.

Spiced Cauliflower in Tomato

SERVES 4—6

(KOUNOUPIDI YIAHNI)

Cauliflower, or *kounoupidi*, is usually prepared in one of three ways in Greece: boiled plain and served with olive oil and lemon juice as a warm salad, pickled in vinegar or cooked in tomato sauce. There are several names for the tomato version, *yiahni* being one of them. You might also see it called *Kounoupidi Kapama*.

There are numerous variations, depending on the region and the cook's personal taste, but one common detail among many of these is the use of cinnamon. Here I've added to that and used a few more spices to give a slightly different edge to the dish. It's lovely without them—a splash of lemon works well in the plainer version—but I feel these warm spices bring out the flavor of the cauliflower in a very interesting and unique way.

¾ cup (110 g) finely chopped onion, lightly packed

2 lb (900 g) potatoes, cut into small pieces

2½ lb (1.1 kg) cauliflower, cut into large florets

6 tbsp (90 ml) olive oil, divided

1 (28-oz [740-g]) can diced tomatoes, no salt added, with liquid

2 bay leaves

1½ tsp (9 g) salt

½ tsp freshly ground black pepper

½ tsp sugar

¼ tsp cinnamon

¼ tsp nutmeg

⅛ tsp allspice

Crusty bread, to serve

Spread the onions over the bottom of the slow cooker insert. Add the potatoes in another layer, then place the cauliflower pieces on top. Drizzle with 2 tablespoons (30 ml) of the olive oil.

Pour half of the tomatoes onto the cauliflower, add the bay leaves, then mix the salt and pepper, sugar, cinnamon, nutmeg and allspice into the remaining half of the tomatoes in the can. Pour the spiced mixture evenly over the contents of the slow cooker. Do not stir. Drizzle with the remaining 4 tablespoons (60 ml) of olive oil.

Cook on low for 5 to 6 hours, or until the potatoes and cauliflower are cooked through and have taken on a red hue. The liquid should be saucy. Remove and discard the bay leaves, then stir gently so as not to crush the cauliflower.

Serve with crusty bread.

PERFECTLY SLOW COOKED, RUSTIC LEGUMES

AH, THE HUMBLE LEGUME! Dried beans, lentils, peas, chickpeas

. . . so many different types to choose from. So nutritious, tasty and filling. Any country that has suffered years of hardship has a significant wealth of legume recipes. Makes sense, right?

Greece produces a lot of legumes. We have some very good brands and very good recipes for soups, stews, mezze, salads . . . you name it. Legumes are very common regardless of the season. They are, of course, the stars of Lent, together with the many delicious vegetables that grow in this country, and people who fast turn to them for their protein and their ability to fill up a hungry tummy.

On warmer days, plain boiled lentils and chickpeas are enjoyed in salads with rice or bulgur wheat, and black-eyed peas are classically paired with chopped parsley and veggies. One can easily make plain legumes in the slow cooker instead of boiling them on the stove, just by cooking them in stock with an onion. Once they are cooked through and soft, they can be drained, portioned, stored in the freezer and enjoyed in a salad when the mood strikes. (If using red kidney beans, check online for instructions as they need special handling.)

When it comes to legumes, salads are all very well, but on cold winter days it's a hearty bowl of soup or stew that Greeks crave. These are the recipes that best suit the slow cooker and are the most famous worldwide, so they are the ones we'll talk about in this chapter.

Before we do, please keep in mind that dried legumes can be very finicky and temperamental. If you get a good batch, it can cook nicely in a logical amount of time. Sometimes, however, you can get a batch that just doesn't want to cooperate. These guys can take hours to reach the consistency that Greeks want for their beans and lentils. That is, soft, buttery and almost falling apart. This happens with all cooking methods, as I'm sure you know. With the slow cooker it just becomes a bit more obvious, so keep it

Fluffy Greek Fava Dip with Onions

(FAVA)

SERVES 6—8

Before anything else, I think I should clarify a couple of things about *Fava* which might be confusing. First and foremost, Greek fava legumes are totally different from what other countries refer to as fava beans, or broad beans. Greek fava is the seed of the plant *lathyrus clymentum* and is native to the Mediterranean. The most famous variety is that of *Santorini*, which is quite unique in quality due to the volcanic nature of the island. *Lathyrus clymentum*, however, is also cultivated in other areas of Greece. In many recipes you will see fava translated as "yellow split peas." Now, I'm no expert on legumes, but I think this is also inaccurate, as peas are in fact a different species (*pisum sativum*). But don't hold me to it. Phew, translating food terms can be a complicated business.

The important thing to know is that Greek fava dip is delicious. It can be made quite chunky or nice and velvety and it's always served with onions. Make it easily in the slow cooker and enjoy as a mezze with bread, like we usually do, or use it in sandwiches. It's also very good as a side dish for a fish- or seafood-based meal.

¾ cup (100 g) carrot, sliced to ¼-inch (6-mm) thickness

1¼ cups (170 g) finely chopped onion, lightly packed

1 lb (450 g) Greek fava legumes (not to be confused with fava beans!)

¼ cup (60 ml) olive oil, plus extra, to serve

1 tsp dried thyme, not coarse

1 bay leaf

½ tsp salt

½ tsp black pepper

4 cups (960 ml) hot vegetable stock

Hot water, as needed

Capers, sliced onions, parsley and lemon wedges, to serve

Place the carrots and onions in the slow cooker pot.

Add the fava legumes, olive oil, thyme, bay leaf, salt, pepper and vegetable stock.

Cook on low for 3 to 5 hours. After the first 2 hours, check it occasionally in case it has absorbed all the liquid. If it has, add small quantities of hot water, ½ cup (120 ml) at a time.

The fava is ready when the legumes are completely soft and falling apart, and the liquid has been mostly absorbed. It might already be quite mushy and that is fine.

Turn the slow cooker off, remove and discard the bay leaf and blend the fava with a stick blender until very smooth. It might seem too runny, like a very thick soup, but it will thicken significantly as it cools. Let it come to room temperature.

Serve with a drizzle of olive oil, a scattering of capers, some sliced onion and some chopped parsley. Accompany with lemon wedges so everyone can squeeze as much as they like on their own portion.

Note: Search for Greek fava legumes online using the terms "Greek fava buy online." You might see them called fava peas too. If you can't find them, you can prepare this dish using yellow split peas in place of the Greek fava legumes, although the result will be slightly different.

Oven-Style Giant Beans in Tomato Sauce

(GIGANTES FOURNOU)

Gigantes is another world-famous legume dish of Greece. The name, which means "giants," is also the name of the large dried white beans used to make it. Gigantes are a variety of the scarlet runner bean. You might see them called butter or lima beans, and although they aren't the same, these could possibly make good alternatives. I haven't tried them myself, but many non-Greek Gigantes recipes call for these instead. My advice is to try to find the real thing online.

Although frequently enjoyed as a main dish, Gigantes also make a great mezze. They are served warm or at room temperature, often alongside feta, olives and smoked meats, cured fish or fried country-style sausage.

1 lb (450 g) dried Greek Gigantes beans

1¼ cups (170 g) finely chopped onion, lightly packed

⅔ cup (85 g) carrot, sliced to ¼-inch (6-mm) thickness

½ cup (60 g) celery, sliced to ¼-inch (6-mm) thickness

1¼ cups (170 g) finely chopped red bell pepper

1 clove garlic, minced

½ cup (120 ml) olive oil, divided

2 bay leaves

1 tsp smoked paprika

1½ tsp (6 g) sugar

½ tsp salt

½ tsp black pepper

2 cups (480 ml) tomato passata (see Notes)

¼ cup (15 g) finely chopped parsley, tightly packed

3 cups (720 ml) water, room temperature

Feta cheese, crusty bread and Kalamata olives, to serve

Soak the beans in a large bowl of water. The water level should be much higher than the level of the beans because they will expand. Leave them for 8 to 10 hours or overnight, before draining.

Combine the onions, carrots, celery, red bell peppers and garlic in the bottom of the slow cooker. Stir ¼ cup (60 ml) of the olive oil into the vegetables. Add the drained beans and bay leaves on top. Mix the smoked paprika, sugar, salt and pepper into the passata and pour evenly over the beans. Sprinkle the parsley on top, pour the water over everything and then drizzle in the rest of the olive oil.

Cook on high for 7 to 8 hours, stirring a couple of times during cooking if possible, until the beans are very soft but not disintegrating. The sauce should be runny but not watery. Prop the lid open by inserting the handle of a wooden spoon under one side, and let the beans cook for 30 to 45 minutes, or until the sauce has thickened. You should be able to see the bottom of the slow cooker for a second when stirring the beans.

Remove and discard the bay leaves, and serve warm or at room temperature with lots of feta cheese, crusty bread and Kalamata olives on the side.

Notes: Don't omit the smoked paprika, or substitute sweet paprika. The smokiness makes this dish extra special.

Tomato passata is a medium-thick juice made of crushed and strained raw tomatoes. You should be able to find it in local stores or Greek markets, or online. You could also use a tomato puree in place of the passata, though results may vary due to some differences in water content and volume.

Set-and-Forget White Bean and Vegetable Soup

(FASOLADA)

SERVES 6—8

Fasolada, for me, means cold weather and mountains. This may be because the first memory I have of eating it is on a weekend getaway with the scouts, during which we visited a mountain lodge and got snowed in. So exciting for a bunch of eight-year-olds!

Despite the connotations Fasolada has for me personally, it's made in all areas of the country, not only those at high altitude. There are many variations, but the most popular is the one with tomato and vegetables. The tricks to perfecting this soup are also plentiful, as getting the consistency right can be a little tricky and depends largely on the beans themselves. The slow cooker, however, makes everything much easier. The low heat means the beans cook nicely, and the blender secret shared below ensures that the soup thickens as it should. As soon as the weather turns and you feel a crispness in the air, soak some beans and make Fasolada. It will warm you like a cozy log fire in a mountain lodge.

1 lb (450 g) navy beans, soaked in water for at least 10 hours

1 cup (140 g) carrots, sliced to ¼-inch (6-mm) thickness

1 cup (110 g) celery ribs without leaves, sliced to ¼-inch (6-mm) thickness

¾ cup (110 g) finely chopped onion, lightly packed

6 cups (1.4 L) hot water

1 (28-oz [740-g]) can diced tomatoes, no salt added, with liquid

2 tbsp (30 ml) tomato paste

2½ tsp (15 g) salt

2 tsp (4 g) sweet paprika

2 tsp (4 g) dried oregano

1 tsp dried thyme

1 tsp black pepper

1 tsp sugar

¾ cup (180 ml) olive oil, divided

Barley rusks (paximadia) or crusty bread, to serve

Feta cheese, to serve

Soak the beans overnight in plenty of fresh water.

Drain the beans and transfer them to the slow cooker insert. Add the carrots, celery, onion, hot water, tomatoes, tomato paste, salt, paprika, oregano, thyme, pepper, sugar and ½ cup (120 ml) of the olive oil.

Stir and cook on low for 7 to 9 hours, or until the beans are very soft. Using a stick blender, pulse two or three times for one second. This will thicken the soup nicely. Add the remaining ¼ cup (60 ml) of olive oil and stir.

Break some barley rusks into your serving bowls and pour the hot soup on top. Or just serve them on the side with the feta cheese. If you aren't using rusks, serve the soup with crusty bread.

Note: Barley rusks (*paximadia* in Greek) are thick pieces of double-baked bread. They are hard and crunchy, and keep very well. Search for them online or in Greek delis/ Mediterranean markets.

Greek Lentil Soup, Frugal and Delicious

(FAKES SOUPA)

SERVES 4

When I was little, you could ask any child anywhere in Greece what their least favorite food was and the answer, 99 times out of 100, would be *Fakes*. When Greeks say "fakes," the word for lentils, they mean this soup, or something very similar to it, as it's the most common way to cook them. I don't know what it is that makes kids dislike the soup, maybe the color or the texture, but I do know that once grown up, almost all of them change their tune. A warm bowl of Fakes with lots of vinegar and a good chunk of feta on the side is one of the best dinners you can wish for on a cold day.

1 lb (450 g) large brown lentils

4 cups (960 ml) hot vegetable stock

4 cups (960 ml) hot water

1 medium onion, minced, or halved if you want to remove it later

3 tbsp (45 ml) olive oil

1 tbsp (15 ml) tomato paste

1 bay leaf

1 tsp salt

1 tsp powdered cumin

½ tsp black pepper

Red wine vinegar, crusty bread and feta cheese, to serve

Combine the lentils, vegetable stock, water, onion, olive oil, tomato paste, bay leaf, salt, cumin and pepper in the slow cooker insert and stir well.

Cook on low for 6 to 7 hours, or until the soup is thick and the lentils are starting to fall apart. For a long while it will look like water with lentils in it, but suddenly it will look like soup. Wait for that.

Remove and discard the bay leaf and serve with a good splash of red wine vinegar (or two!), lots of crusty bread and lots of feta cheese. Personally, I like to crumble feta on top so that it imparts its flavor into the soup. Don't skip it for this recipe!

Note: While cooking, a dark brown/black film might develop on the surface of the soup. This is okay; just stir it back in.

Hearty, Traditional Chickpea Stew with Rosemary

(REVITHADA)

SERVES 4—6

Chickpea stews and soups are very common in Greece. There is one particular version, though, that is very special. *Revithada* from Sifnos is unique, both in its use of a mere handful of ingredients and in the way it's cooked. Sifnos is an island famous for its clay ceramics, and one of the utensils traditionally made is a large pot with a lid called *skepastaria*. The chickpea stew ingredients are combined in this pot and cooked in a wood oven overnight at low heat. So, you see I just had to try it in the slow cooker!

As I mentioned, the original recipe has very few ingredients, but their good quality is of vital importance to the success of the dish—especially the chickpeas themselves and the olive oil, of which there is a significant amount. The rest of the original ingredients are onions, bay leaves, salt and lemon to serve. In this version, I've chosen to add a bit of rosemary (not an uncommon addition for this dish and a delicious one too) and some vegetable stock to give some extra depth to the overall flavor.

---

1 lb (450 g) dried chickpeas, fresh and of good quality

1 tbsp (15 g) dried rosemary

2 tsp (12 g) salt

1 tsp freshly ground black pepper

1 large onion, halved (see Notes)

2 bay leaves

½ cup (120 ml) olive oil

3 cups (720 ml) hot vegetable stock

1¼ cups (300 ml) hot water

Freshly squeezed lemon juice and fresh crusty bread, to serve

Soak the chickpeas overnight in plenty of fresh water, for 10 to 12 hours.

In the morning, drain the chickpeas (they will have expanded), rinse them with fresh water, drain again and transfer them to the slow cooker.

Add the rosemary, salt, pepper, onion halves and bay leaves. Drizzle with the olive oil. Pour the vegetable stock and water over everything and cook on low for 7 to 9 hours. The stew is ready when the chickpeas are cooked through and fall-apart tender, but not disintegrating. The liquid in the pot should be slightly thickened.

Remove and discard the bay leaves and serve with a squeeze of lemon juice and lots of crusty bread to dunk in the stew.

Notes: Cooking times for chickpeas may vary hugely. They depend very much on the quality of the legumes and the freshness. Allow for extra time, so that if your chickpeas aren't ready within the hours stated, you can extend the cooking time until they are nicely softened and buttery.

I prefer to add the onion halved so it imparts its flavor, but can easily be removed at the end. If you prefer, you can chop it finely before cooking.

One-Pot Black-Eyed Beans with Beet Greens

(MAVROMATIKA ME HORTA)

This dish is a great example of how similar certain dishes can be, even though they are from opposite sides of the globe. Beans and greens are a popular combination here in Greece, just as they are—surprisingly, to us—in the southern United States.

Black-eyed beans are a lovely legume. They don't need soaking, they are very tasty and they work brilliantly in the slow cooker. After seeing how beautifully beet greens cook in it too, I decided I would try a combination of these two ingredients. The result is an easy, nutritious, intensely flavorful dish.

6 tbsp (90 ml) olive oil, divided

¾ cup (110 g) finely chopped onion, lightly packed

¾ lb (350 g) dried black-eyed beans

1¼ cups (225 g) finely chopped fresh tomato

1½ lb (680 g) beet greens, stalks included, roughly chopped into 3 to 4 pieces

1 tsp salt

½ tsp freshly ground black pepper

4 cups (960 ml) hot vegetable stock

Feta cheese and fresh bread, to serve

Add 2 tablespoons (30 ml) of the olive oil to the slow cooker insert and layer the onion, beans, tomato, beet greens, salt, pepper and vegetable stock in the insert. Don't be alarmed at the quantity of the greens; just press them down and they will wilt significantly during cooking. Drizzle the remaining 4 tablespoons (60 ml) of olive oil on top of everything.

Cook on low for 5 to 7 hours, or until the beans and beet green stalks are soft. Serve with a little bit of the sauce from the pot.

Enjoy with feta cheese and lots of fresh bread.

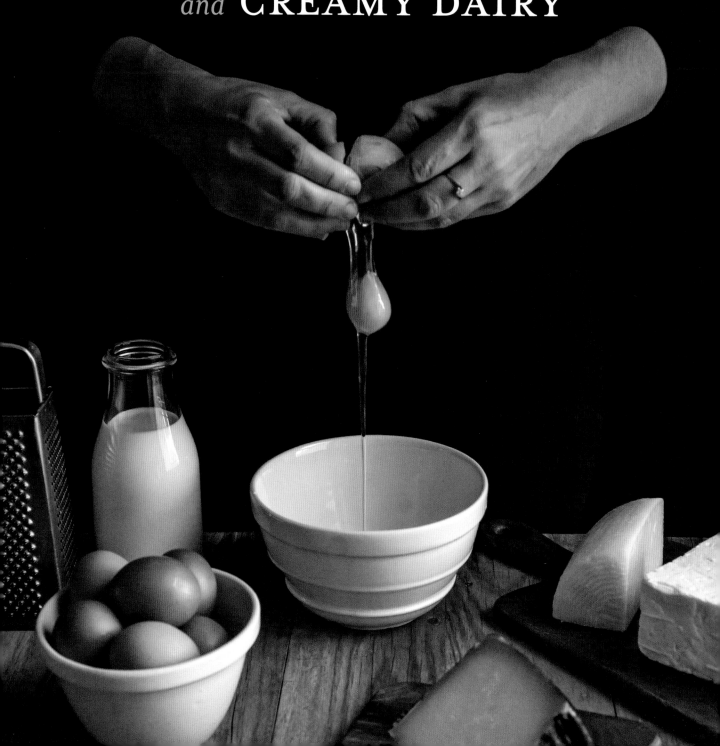

I HAVE TO ADMIT that I don't think I could live without eggs and dairy products. In fact, as I write these lines, I am munching on a cheese sandwich. And no, it's not a feta sandwich!

When it comes to dairy, two of the most famous products in the whole world are Greek feta cheese and Greek yogurt. Dairy in general holds a special place in Greek cuisine. Our huge variety of delicious cheeses made from sheep, goat and cow's milk include Gruyères, hard yellow cheeses, smoked cheeses, fresh soft white cheeses, dry white cheeses . . . the list goes on. Strained yogurt (which is what Greek yogurt is called here) is very popular of course, but so are a multitude of other types, like sheep's yogurt which is slightly sweet and quite creamy, and goat's yogurt, which is wonderfully tangy. In terms of drinking milk, it's usually from cows nowadays, although goat's milk is still fairly widely consumed.

I have to add here that a few decades ago, it was very common for children to be given evaporated milk to drink in the morning. I think the high percentage of Greeks who hate milk and never drink it might be a direct result of this. It's my own theory, but I truly believe it cannot be unrelated. Having said that, I have a new-found respect for evaporated milk now that I'm an adult—not for drinking but for cooking. And you might be interested to know that it behaves very well in the slow cooker!

Apart from dairy, eggs also play an important role in Greek cuisine, with fresh eggs "from the village" being a highly sought-after commodity, especially for those who have children. In fact, you don't have to travel far outside the capital to reach areas where some homes have their own chicken coops.

In terms of the slow cooker, most manuals tell us that dairy products aren't quite suited to it and should be added at the end. Eggs don't often feature in such recipes either. Indeed, foods like omelets and milky, cheesy sauces aren't the first things that come to mind when thinking of your slow cooker, am I right? Well, once again, the slow cooker proves it has more tricks up its proverbial sleeve.

From milky trahana soup to creamy, cheesy pasta and hearty, chunky omelets, the recipes that follow may well surprise you.

Country-Style Sausage and Potato Omelet

(FRUTALIA ANDROU)

This recipe is a personal favorite. The idea for making it hit me one day like a bolt of lightning. I was already a fan of slow cooker "baked" potatoes, slow cooker frittatas and slow cooker sausages, but hadn't thought to combine them. Then, during the research stage of this book and while I was thinking of potential recipes, I stumbled on *Frutalia*. Frutalia is an omelet originating from the island of Andros, made with fried potatoes and sausages. I knew of the dish—it's quite famous here—but dismissed it as a candidate because frying everything first then using the slow cooker only to cook the egg seemed a bit pointless. A few days later, while walking the dog, it came to me out of the blue. Why not use the slow cooker for both stages? Cook the potatoes and sausages first, then chop them and make the omelet! No extra washing up, no smelly and calorie-loaded frying; just a delicious dish perfect for lunch, dinner or a filling snack. I am thrilled that it worked out so well.

You can go about this recipe in two ways. Cook the potatoes and sausages while you work during the day, then finish the dish off by making the omelet for dinner. Or, cook the potatoes and sausages during the night and make the omelet in the morning. It would also make a great brunch dish!

---

2 lb (900 g) whole baby potatoes, skin on

1 lb (450 g), or 4 small raw Greek country-style pork sausages, whole (see Note)

½ cup (60 g) coarsely grated Gruyère cheese from Crete, or your favorite hard yellow cheese, tightly packed, divided

9 eggs

6 tbsp (90 ml) milk

1½ tsp (1 g) dried spearmint

½ tsp salt

½ tsp freshly ground black pepper

Stage one

Put the potatoes in the bottom of the slow cooker and place the whole sausages on top without any additional ingredients. Cook on low for 6 to 8 hours, or until the sausages are cooked through and the potatoes are tender; a sharp knife should easily glide through the largest one. Remove and set aside until ready to make the omelet.

Stage two

Make a sling for the insert following the instructions on page 11.

Slice the cooked sausages and potatoes into rounds. Lay half the potato slices on the bottom of the slow cooker insert, on the paper. Then lay half the sausage slices on top of the potatoes. Sprinkle with half the cheese. Repeat the layers with the second half of the potatoes, sausages and cheese.

Beat the eggs with the milk in a bowl and add the spearmint, salt and pepper. Pour over the layers in the slow cooker insert, trying to get the mixture into the cracks so it reaches the bottom. Move the insert slowly in a circling motion so the liquid is distributed evenly.

Cook on low for 2 to 3 hours, or until the surface is set and a knife comes out clean when inserted in the center of the omelet. Let cool for 5 minutes. Carefully remove the omelet by pulling the foil "handles." Slice and serve with a large green salad.

> **Note:** Look for raw Greek sausages in Greek delis or markets. Alternatively, use strong flavored raw Italian-style sausages.

Retro Greek Macaroni and Cheese with Cream

(MAKARONIA SOUFLE)

There are three main pasta dishes I remember distinctly from my childhood and teenage years, and to my recollection they were the most popular at the time: spaghetti with meat sauce, pasta with tomato sauce and pasta "carbonara." I have put the word carbonara in quotation marks so my Italian friends don't stop talking to me, as what was then known as carbonara is, well . . . not quite the real thing. No egg to be found anywhere, no pancetta—usually not even bacon, just ham—and lots and lots of cream. It was actually very good, although that might be nostalgia speaking.

Apart from those three dishes, another hugely popular creation was the inexplicably named "pasta soufflé." This superstar was reserved for parties and special occasions. A big baking dish would be filled with boiled pasta, heaps of melty cheeses, cubed ham and cream, then cooked until golden. It was a favorite centerpiece for a festive table, especially during the eighties. The love child of these retro "carbonara" and "soufflé" dishes is this creamy slow cooker macaroni and cheese with ham. The pasta is cooked right there in the pot, so no extra washing up and no extra effort is required. Easy enough for a midweek dinner, but indulgent enough for a special occasion!

---

3 tbsp (45 ml) olive oil, divided

1 lb (450 g) penne pasta, uncooked

1 lb (450 g) smoked ham, cubed

2 cups (200 g) coarsely grated gouda cheese

2 cups (200 g) coarsely grated kasseri cheese (see Note)

4 cups (960 ml) plus ⅓ cup (80 ml) whole milk, divided, plus extra if needed during cooking

1⅓ cups (320 ml) heavy cream

1 tbsp (15 ml) prepared yellow mustard

1½ tsp (2 g) dried thyme

1 tsp salt

1 tsp freshly ground black pepper

¾ tsp garlic powder

½ tsp nutmeg

Green salad, to serve

Drizzle 1 tablespoon (15 ml) of the olive oil into the bottom of the slow cooker insert. Add half the pasta and scatter half of the ham on top. Sprinkle with half of the gouda cheese and half of the kasseri cheese, then repeat the layers of pasta, ham and cheese. Drizzle the remaining oil over the top.

Whisk 4 cups (960 ml) of the milk with the rest of the ingredients in a bowl and pour over the contents of the slow cooker.

Cook on low for 1½ to 2½ hours, or until the pasta is cooked through and the cheese is completely melted. If at any time during cooking you see that the liquid has been absorbed yet the pasta is uncooked, add small amounts of extra milk and stir.

When ready, turn the slow cooker off and stir in the remaining ⅓ cup (80 ml) of milk to give the pasta some extra moisture. Keep in mind it will thicken as it rests. If you aren't serving it straight away, prop the lid open.

Serve as a main course along with a green salad, or as a side to a grilled meat dish.

Note: If you can't find kasseri cheese at your local grocer, try Greek markets or online sources, or try the dish with cheddar for a slightly different flavor.

Spicy "Baked" Feta Cheese Parcels

(BOUYIOURDI)

One of my mum's favorites, this recipe makes a great little mezze. If you've never tried feta in its baked form, it's definitely worth doing so. It may or may not melt depending on the feta you are using, but either way, its flavor turns into something wonderful.

The word *Bouyiourdi*, apart from this delightful appetizer, also means (in slang) a bill or notice of payment of some sort. According to many of the explanations online, it comes from the Turkish word *buyruk* which means "order" or "command." Since commands from officers of the Ottoman Empire were bad news during the Turkish occupation of Greece, the word came to have this negative connotation. Some say the dish Bouyiourdi took this name because of the spiciness (bad news) it brings to the taste buds.

The level of spiciness in this version is definitely not bad news, as it's fairly mild and in any case, easily adaptable. Make some Bouyiourdi as a mezze for a party, an appetizer to share or even a side dish to grilled meat.

---

4 (12 x 8-inch [30 x 20-cm]) pieces of aluminum foil

4 (12 x 8-inch [30 x 20-cm]) pieces of parchment paper

1 lb (450 g) feta cheese, cut into 4 wide slices

1 plum tomato, sliced into rounds

1 medium roasted red pepper from a jar (preserved in brine), drained well and roughly chopped

¼ cup (40 g) hot green chili pepper (or to taste), finely chopped

½ cup (60 g) kasseri cheese, cut into ½-inch (1.3-cm) cubes

4 tsp (20 ml) olive oil

1 tsp oregano

½ tsp sweet paprika or to taste

½ tsp chili flakes or to taste

Warm toasted bread, to serve

Lay the foil squares on a work surface and cover each one with a piece of parchment paper.

Place a slice of feta on each square. Divide the tomato, roasted red pepper and green chili pepper between the four slices, layering them on top.

Divide the kasseri cubes over the top and drizzle each square with 1 teaspoon of the olive oil. Sprinkle ¼ teaspoon of oregano, ⅛ teaspoon of paprika and ⅛ teaspoon of chili flakes on each of the four squares.

Bring the sides of the squares up and seal on top. Transfer the parcels to the slow cooker insert. It's okay if they don't all fit in one layer, but don't squash them.

Cook on high for 1 to 2 hours, or until the kasseri cheese has melted and the feta, tomato and chili peppers have softened. The parcels should be fragrant and steaming hot.

Serve immediately with warm toasted bread to dip in the juices.

Greek Summer Scrambled Eggs

(STRAPATSADA)

Name a sunny country and I'm willing to bet they have an egg and tomato recipe of some type. *Shakshouka* from the Middle East (or North Africa; its origin is disputed), *menemen* from Turkey, huevos rancheros from Mexico, stir-fried tomato and scrambled eggs from China, eggs in purgatory from Italy . . . the list goes on. Here, we have our own tomato and egg dish called *Strapatsada*, or *Kayanas*. The third ingredient is—you guessed it— feta cheese. But of course!

Strapatsada (which comes from the Italian *strapazzare*, meaning to scramble, mistreat, bash around, handle roughly . . . you get the picture) is a summer dish, usually eaten for breakfast or as a snack. It's one of those that, for many Greeks, brings back memories of summer mornings with Grandma lovingly making breakfast before allowing them to go out and play with the neighborhood kids, or of quick lunches on hot afternoons after returning from the beach.

The versions and methods of making Strapatsada are numerous, but this slow cooker recipe is definitely one of the simplest. As an added bonus, you can use the seeds and juices of the tomatoes to drizzle over some toasted bread for serving. Of course, you'll need tasty ripe tomatoes for this recipe.

¼ cup (60 ml) olive oil, divided, plus extra for bread

2 lb (900 g) plum tomatoes

2 tsp (2 g) onion flakes, or to taste

1 tsp dried basil

1 tsp freshly ground black pepper

¾ tsp dried oregano, plus extra for bread

¼ tsp salt

8 eggs

4–6 slices of crusty or sourdough bread

1½ cups (200 g) feta cheese, crumbled into ½- to 1-inch (1.3- to 2.5-cm) pieces

A few pinches of oregano

Fleur de sel or coarse sea salt

Use 2 tablespoons (30 ml) of the olive oil to generously coat the slow cooker insert. Make sure to come up the sides and don't miss any spots because egg tends to stick.

Quarter the tomatoes and squeeze them over a bowl so that the seeds and juices fall out. Make sure to get all the "pockets" of the tomato open, teasing with a sharp knife if necessary. Set the juices and seeds aside. Chop the remaining flesh roughly (it should come to about 4 cups [650 g]), and transfer it to the slow cooker insert.

Stir the onion flakes, dried basil, black pepper, oregano and salt into the tomatoes.

Beat the eggs in a bowl until smooth and pour them over the tomatoes in the slow cooker. Drizzle with the remaining olive oil and prod the mixture in places so the eggs become incorporated. Cook on low for 1½ to 2 hours, breaking up the mixture a couple of times during cooking, if desired. You can do this at the end if you prefer.

While the eggs are cooking, preheat the broiler in your oven and line a baking tray with aluminum foil. Lay the bread on the foil, place it under the broiler and lightly toast on one side until golden. Remove the tray, flip the bread and lightly brush the non-toasted side with olive oil. Broil for a few more minutes until toasted.

The eggs are ready when they have set, and any juices in the pot are clear. It's important not to overcook them, so keep an eye on them depending on how hot your slow cooker runs. They will continue to cook slightly even after turned off. After breaking up the eggs, sprinkle in the feta and stir gently.

Transfer the toasted bread onto a platter, sprinkle with a few pinches of oregano and fleur de sel, and drizzle with the juices and seeds you saved from the tomatoes, if desired. Serve the eggs with the bread on the side.

Creamy, Nourishing Trahana Soup

(TRAHANAS)

You may remember this weird and wonderful ingredient from the Crustless Zucchini "Pie" with Trahanas (Kolokythopita me Trahana) over on page 113. This thick, creamy, delicious soup, however, is the most common way to prepare trahanas here in Greece. Nowadays you may come across modern creations such as *trahanoto* (a risotto-like dish), but the soup is what springs to most Greeks' minds when they hear the word "trahanas".

I was very late to the trahanas game, for two specific reasons. The first is that my mum hates it. So, there was no way she was ever going to cook it for us when we were children. The second is that my first encounter with it was when I was about ten and I entered a room in which there was freshly made trahanas drying out on a large sheet. Oh, my goodness! The smell made me flee. It took years to build up the courage to try it. But when I did, I couldn't believe how amazingly delicious and comforting the taste was. Although pretty intense, in no way did it remind me of that horrific encounter. Maybe it smells so strongly only when it's drying, or maybe my memory created a monster out of nothing. One thing is for sure—I'm making up for lost time with this one. Especially now that I've created this easy, deliciously creamy slow cooker version of trahana soup.

---

1 cup (170 g) sour trahana

7 cups (1.7 L) hot vegetable stock

1 cup (240 ml) evaporated milk

½ tsp salt

½ tsp black pepper

2 tbsp (30 g) butter

For the croutons

4 pieces of stale bread, cut into small cubes

Olive oil spray

1-2 pinches of dried thyme

1-2 pinches of salt

Feta cheese, to serve

Sumac, to serve (see Notes)

Combine the trahana, vegetable stock, milk, salt, pepper and butter in the slow cooker insert and cook on low for 1½ to 2 hours. The longer the soup cooks, the thicker it will become, so let it reach a consistency you like.

Lay the cubes of bread on a baking tray lined with grease-proof paper. Spray the cubes with a little olive oil and sprinkle with the thyme and salt. Bake in a pre-heated oven at 300°F (150°C), for 10 to 15 minutes, or until the bread is golden, crunchy and fragrant. Remove the croutons from the oven and let them cool.

Serve the soup with crumbled feta, croutons and a sprinkling of sumac.

Notes: If you are worried the flavor might be too strong, you could try the soup with a sweet trahanas first. Then, if you like that, move on to a sour variety. Look for it online or in Greek delis.

Sumac is a Middle Eastern spice that suits trahanas very well. Look for it online or in Middle Eastern delis.

If you have leftovers, you can easily reheat them, adding a splash of water to thin the soup.

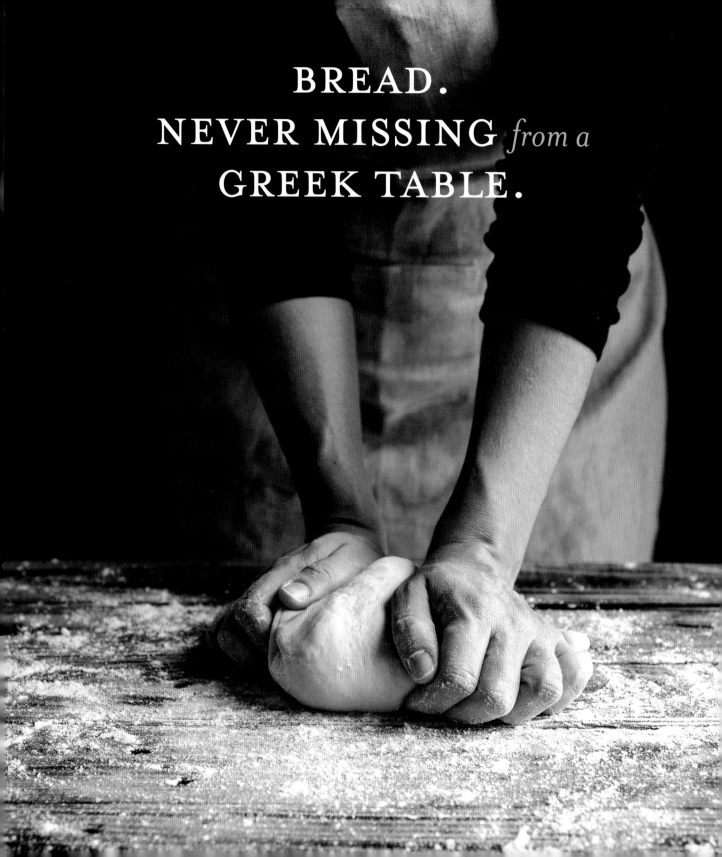

BREAD.
NEVER MISSING *from a*
GREEK TABLE.

table, whether in a restaurant or our own homes, and it's bought fresh every day. As a result, bakeries are plentiful in every single city neighborhood, town or village. There are few things better than breaking a big hunk of bread off a loaf, hot out of a bakery oven.

The Mister tells a story of how when he was a child, his mother would send him to buy bread, only to receive a quarter of a loaf by the time he got back. She eventually started giving him money for two loaves, one for him and one for the rest of the family. Even today, the only time he doesn't eat bread with his dinner is when we're having pizza.

The recipes that follow aren't for your typical everyday bread. I've chosen something a bit different. Yeast bread that both rises and "bakes" in the slow cooker, brown soda bread made with an ancient grain called Zea (Emmer wheat) and savory corn bread.

They are all delicious and they are all made in the slow cooker! How cool is that?

Sun-Dried Tomato and Oregano Yeast Bread

(KARVELI ME LIASTI)

SERVES 6—8

I think the star of this recipe is the tip for how you can use the slow cooker not only to "bake" it, but also to let it rise beforehand. The bread itself is a simple round white loaf speckled with bits of sun-dried tomato and a sprinkling of oregano to complete the rustic aromas. It's great as an accompaniment to a meal and can also be served on its own, with some cheese, or with butter.

3⅓ cups (450 g) all-purpose flour, lightly packed, divided

½ cup (30 g) sun-dried tomatoes, completely dry (not oil preserved), very finely chopped, tightly packed

1½ tsp (3 g) dried oregano

1 tsp salt

1 tsp sugar

1 packet instant dry yeast (see Note)

2 tbsp (30 ml) plus ½ tsp olive oil, divided

1 cup (240 ml) warm water (about 90°F [32°C])

Note: I have not mentioned a specific quantity for the yeast, as the strength may vary from brand to brand and country to country. So check the package for details on how much you need for this amount of flour.

Sprinkle ¼ teaspoon of the flour over the sun-dried tomatoes and toss to coat. Set aside.

Put the remaining flour in a large bowl with the oregano and stir with a whisk. With your finger, make a well in the middle of the flour. Carefully sprinkle the salt around the edges of the flour, near the sides of the bowl, so that it doesn't go into the well. Put the sugar and yeast directly into the well, add 2 tablespoons (30 ml) of the olive oil and then slowly pour in the warm water. Stir with a wooden spoon starting from the center. When the dough starts coming together, switch to mixing with your hands. Add the sun-dried tomato pieces and knead well with your hands for 10 to 12 minutes, working the dough on a flat surface.

Find a deep heatproof bowl that fits in your slow cooker, and lightly grease it with the remaining ½ teaspoon of olive oil. Shape the dough into a ball and place it in the bowl.

Line your slow cooker insert with a few dish towels and put the bowl inside. Make sure the bowl is snugly surrounded by towels, underneath and around the sides. Do not put the lid on but cover the bowl with another clean dish towel. Turn the cooker on the warm setting and let the dough rise for about an hour.

Remove the bowl from the slow cooker, turn the dough out onto a lightly floured surface and knead it gently so as not the push out all the air (no punching!), for 1 minute. Line the same bowl with a large piece of parchment paper and put the dough back inside. Return it to its "nest" in the slow cooker and let it rise again for about 40 to 45 minutes.

Remove the bowl and towels from the slow cooker, and working quickly but very gently, lift the edges of the paper up and transfer the dough up out of the bowl and down into the empty slow cooker insert (with the paper). Don't handle the dough or it will lose air; use the paper to move it.

Tuck the corners of the parchment in by folding toward the sides of the slow cooker. Lay two long pieces of paper towel lengthwise along the top of the insert (side by side, overlapping and leaving no gaps at the sides). Place the lid on to secure them in place so they sit tautly under the lid, without falling in and touching the dough.

Cook on high for 2½ to 3 hours, or until the surface is completely dry and the loaf sounds very hollow when tapped. The underside will be slightly browned. If desired, turn on the broiler and place the bread under it for a few minutes until it browns nicely on the surface. The timing will depend on the strength of your broiler and your preferences as to the color of the bread, so keep watching it. Let the loaf cool completely on a wire rack before cutting.

Emmer Flour Soda Bread with Greek Yogurt and Seeds

(PSOMI ZEAS)

SERVES 8—12

Many things have been said here in Greece about emmer wheat (*Triticum dicoccum*). Widely cultivated in the ancient world, it has become quite the trend to cook with emmer flour in recent years. It even comes with its very own conspiracy theory. According to a handful of people, emmer wheat was banned in recent history for reasons that are connected to its rumored superfood qualities and the ability it has to "unlock" the brain and let it think properly. Yes, the conspiracy theorists believe that other nations (or, um, aliens) somehow intervened so that we couldn't eat emmer flour in Greece, therefore suppressing our genius-ness.

Alas, I cannot say that making this bread will suddenly make you a genius, but it is definitely nutritious and undoubtedly delicious. It's not a traditional Greek recipe, although one does easily find emmer bread in Greece nowadays. In this version, I chose to combine the emmer flour with some of my favorite seeds, giving it an extra boost of flavor and goodness.

Best thing about it? No kneading and no proofing! Try it with butter and honey, or even better, butter, honey and a sharp yellow cheese.

3⅔ cups (510 g) emmer flour, lightly packed

2 tbsp (30 g) flaxseeds

2 tbsp (30 g) sunflower seeds

1 tbsp (15 g) black sesame seeds

1 tbsp (15 g) baking soda

1½ tsp (9 g) salt

¾ cup (200 g) Greek yogurt

1¾ cup plus 2 tbsp (450 ml) water

2 tbsp (30 ml) olive oil

1 tbsp (15 ml) honey

Line your slow cooker insert with a sheet of parchment paper, making sure it reaches up the sides.

In a large bowl, whisk the flour, flaxseeds, sunflower seeds, black sesame seeds, baking soda and salt. Set aside.

Using a separate bowl, whisk together the yogurt, water, olive oil and honey.

Mix the wet ingredients into the dry until well incorporated and pour the mixture onto the parchment in the slow cooker. Smooth out the surface if necessary and place a long piece of paper towel across the top of the insert, under the lid—it should sit there, not fall onto the dough.

Cook on high for 2 to 3 hours, or until the bread sounds hollow when tapped and a skewer or a knife comes out completely clean after being inserted in the center.

Turn out onto a wire rack and let cool completely.

Note: If you can't find emmer flour at major supermarkets in your area, search for it online or at specialty stores.

Flat Corn Bread with Feta and Gruyère Cheese

(BOBOTA)

During the second world war, Greece went through times of extreme poverty. Wheat was in very short supply and since corn was the main crop, cornmeal was used widely for breads and pies.

One of the most popular breads at the time was called *bobota*, also known as "poor man's bread." It was usually made with cornmeal, water and whatever else was available in the pantry.

Nowadays we can afford to re-vamp old recipes like this, so my version has a few more ingredients than its ancestors, giving more complexity to the flavor. Cheese and spearmint suit bobota very well, making it an ideal snack or picnic food, reminiscent of a typical Greek cheese pie, only easier to make. It's super simple to throw together and its distinct flavor and texture make it stand out from regular breads or flatbreads.

---

1 cup (140 g) cornmeal, lightly packed

⅔ cup (85 g) all-purpose flour, lightly packed

1 tsp dried spearmint

1 tsp baking powder

¼ tsp baking soda

¼ tsp salt

¼ tsp freshly ground black pepper

7 tbsp (105 ml) milk

6 tbsp (100 g) Greek yogurt

5 tbsp (75 ml) olive oil

½ cup (60 g) mild Greek Gruyère, coarsely grated, tightly packed (a sweet one works well)

1½ cups (200 g) feta cheese, crumbled into ½- to 1-inch (1.3- to 2.5-cm) pieces

In a large bowl, whisk the cornmeal, flour, spearmint, baking powder, baking soda, salt and pepper.

Whisk the milk, yogurt and olive oil in a separate bowl until smooth and pour it into the dry ingredients. Stir well with a wooden spoon.

Add the grated Gruyère and stir a bit more until almost incorporated. Crumble the feta cheese over the bowl, making sure to leave some larger pieces. Stir gently so as to keep the feta intact as much as possible.

Line the slow cooker insert with a sheet of parchment paper, pressing the edges flat up against the sides of the pot. Transfer the dough to the insert and spread it out with a silicone spatula or your fingers. Flatten it as best you can and lay a long piece of paper towel across the top of the slow cooker. Secure with the lid. Make sure that the paper towel is not touching the dough; it's there to catch the condensation. It's fine if there are gaps at the two long sides of the paper.

Cook on high for 1½ to 2 hours, or until the edges are crispy and beginning to brown and the middle is set.

Holding all four corners, lift the parchment paper up and out of the slow cooker and lay on a cooling rack. Let the bread come to room temperature before serving.

"PIECE *of* CAKE"
SWEETS

I LOVE MAKING SWEET TREATS in the slow cooker. It's a brilliant way to have cake in the summer without making the house an inferno, and it's also great if you can't be checking the oven every two minutes. The window for getting things right in the slow cooker is much bigger, so you have more time in between peeks. Plus, if you like baking often, the slow cooker can keep your electricity bills down.

Greek desserts feature lots of nuts, phyllo pastry, semolina, honey, syrup and spices. In fact, sweets might generally have more spices than savory dishes. Cinnamon is the main player, but other warm spices like cloves also appear frequently. Fruit and milk also play roles in many traditional desserts, especially in pies.

The result you get in the slow cooker for many of these typical Greek sweets is very impressive, and I'm truly happy to be including them in this book.

Deeply Chocolatey Chocolate Cake

(SOKOLATOPITA SYROPIASTI)

My favorite *sokolatopita* was always the one from the bakery near my mum's house. They would strategically place huge trays of it next to the cash register so no one could resist getting a piece or two on the way out.

When I was thinking about dessert recipes for this book, I wanted to include something chocolatey. So, I decided to try and re-create that amazing dessert in the slow cooker. I have to admit it took a few tries, but I got it in the end. This is now, of course, my new favorite. The word "sokolatopita" in Greek literally means chocolate pie. Sometimes we call things pie even if they are more like a tart or a cake, as is this one. Gorgeously moist in texture, attractively dark in color, fabulously chocolatey in flavor . . . call it pie, call it cake, it doesn't really matter. All that matters is that it's delicious and so easy to make.

For the cake

1 tsp instant espresso powder

7 tbsp (105 ml) hot water

1 cup (140 g) all-purpose flour, lightly packed

7 tbsp (70 g) coarse semolina, lightly packed

½ cup (40 g) unsweetened cocoa powder

1 cup (225 g) sugar

2½ tsp (12 g) baking powder

¼ tsp salt

3 eggs

½ cup plus 2 tbsp (150 ml) mild-tasting olive oil

For the syrup

¾ cup (180 ml) water

1 cup (225 g) sugar

⅔ cup (60 g) unsweetened cocoa powder

For the ganache

¾ cup (110 g) dark chocolate, roughly chopped

7 tbsp (105 ml) full fat cream

Strawberries and cream, optional, to serve

To make the cake, stir the espresso powder into the hot water until it dissolves, then let it cool.

Mix the flour, semolina, cocoa powder, sugar, baking powder and salt in a large bowl and set aside. Use a whisk to get rid of lumps.

In a separate medium-sized bowl, beat the eggs and olive oil until smooth.

Prepare a sling for the slow cooker by following the instructions on page 11.

When the espresso has cooled slightly, beat it into the egg and oil mixture.

Whisk the wet ingredients into the dry, until the mixture is smooth and lump-free. Transfer the batter to the slow cooker and cover the insert with a long piece of paper towel, securing it with the lid. The paper should lie tautly under it, without touching the batter. Cook on high for 1½ to 2½ hours, or until the cake looks set on top and a toothpick inserted into the center comes out clean or with dry crumbs. The top might still be sticky so don't test by touching it.

As soon as the cake starts cooking, make the syrup, as it will need to cool before you use it. Bring the water, sugar and cocoa powder to a boil on the stovetop and stir well for a minute or two until the sugar and cocoa dissolve. Set aside until completely cooled.

When the cake is ready and still hot, and the slow cooker has been turned off, poke some holes in the cake with a thin skewer. Slowly spoon the cold syrup all over the cake. Let it sit in order to absorb the chocolatey goodness.

After the syrup-soaked cake has cooled completely, make the ganache. Put the chocolate in a heatproof bowl, add the cream and heat on high in the microwave for 30 seconds. Stir and heat again for another 30 seconds. Let the mixture sit so the chocolate melts completely and stir with a spatula until you get a thick chocolate sauce. Set aside to cool to a spreadable consistency.

Spread the ganache onto the cake and leave it until it sets.

Lift the sokolatopita out of the slow cooker by pulling it up with the foil strips that act as "handles." Cut it into squares and serve with strawberries and cream, if desired.

Greek Sticky Walnut Cake

SERVES 8—10

(KARYDOPITA)

Ah, the beloved *karydopita*. The name comes from the words *karydia,* which means walnuts, and *pita,* which means pie. This is another pie that is more like cake, although it is pretty unique, as there is no flour in it. The main ingredients in most versions are ground walnuts, a type of wheat rusk called "frigania," sugar, cinnamon and eggs. Lots of eggs. After baking, the whole thing is drenched in syrup. It's one of the most popular traditional desserts in Greece and really rather special. What makes mine stand out? Well, it's made in the slow cooker. And works perfectly in it.

1¼ cups plus 2 tbsp (140 g) ground walnuts, processed into coarse, small crumbs (not powder)

⅔ cup (70 g) wheat rusks processed into very fine crumbs, tightly packed

2 tbsp (15 g) powdered cinnamon

¼ tsp cloves

2¼ tsp (10 g) baking powder

⅔ cup (140 g) sugar, divided

8 eggs, separated

1½ tsp (7 ml) vanilla extract

For the syrup

1½ cups (340 g) sugar

1½ cups (360 ml) water

1 tbsp (15 ml) freshly squeezed lemon juice

1 stick cinnamon

Prepare a sling for the slow cooker as per the instructions on page 11.

Using a whisk, stir the processed walnuts, rusk crumbs, cinnamon, cloves and baking powder in a bowl.

Reserve 1 tablespoon (12 g) of the sugar and beat the rest with the egg yolks on high speed until very pale in color, for about 5 minutes, scraping down the sides of the bowl often. Add the vanilla and beat until incorporated. Fold in the walnut mixture with a spatula.

In a very clean bowl, using clean beaters on your mixer, beat the egg whites with the reserved tablespoon (12 g) of sugar until the resulting meringue forms stiff peaks, about 6 to 7 minutes.

Very gently fold half the meringue into the batter and repeat with the second half.

Transfer the mixture to the slow cooker, cover with a paper towel—the paper should not touch the batter, only lie tautly under the lid to catch condensation—and cook on high for 1½ to 2 hours, or until the surface is set and a toothpick comes out clean when inserted in the center of the cake.

As soon as the cake starts cooking, make the syrup so it has time to cool. Bring the sugar, water, lemon juice and cinnamon to a boil in a small saucepan. Turn to medium-high and let everything bubble for 5 minutes. Set aside.

When ready, turn the slow cooker off and immediately start spooning the cold syrup slowly over the hot cake, while still in the pot. Do this one spoonful at a time, so the cake has time to absorb it. Discard the cinnamon stick.

Let the cake cool completely, remove using the sling "handles," cut it into small diamond shaped pieces and serve. Keep in mind karydopita is better on the second day.

Notes: Keep the cake in the slow cooker insert for the first day and flip it upside down for a while if the syrup collects at the bottom.

Wheat rusks can be found online or at Greek delis. They are called *frigania* in Greek. You might see them called "thin white rusks," "thin wheat rusks" or "golden rusks." Although wheat rusks are ideal, you could also try plain melba toast (use ⅔ cup [70 g], lightly packed), processed into fine, powdery crumbs.

Fragrant Orange Phyllo Pie

(PORTOKALOPITA)

This *Portokalopita*, or rather the fact that it works so well in the slow cooker, fascinates me. The first time I made it I couldn't believe how gorgeously it turned out, especially considering how tricky it is to cook pastry at low temperatures. To give credit where credit is due, the fact that I even tried it is down to my friend Constantina. It's a recipe she has been using for years. Unlike most Greek orange pies, it doesn't have yogurt or juice and the intense orange flavor comes solely from zest. I had my doubts that it would work in the slow cooker, but Constantina insisted I give it a go. Well, hats off to her, as she certainly knew best!

12 oz (340 g) Greek phyllo pastry dough, thawed if frozen (see Note)

6 tbsp (90 ml) olive oil

6 tbsp (90 ml) sunflower oil, or other neutral vegetable oil

1 cup (225 g) sugar

3 eggs

3 tsp (14 g) baking powder

¾ tsp vanilla extract

1½ tbsp (15 g) fresh orange zest, packed

For the syrup

1½ tbsp (15 g) orange zest, loosely packed

1 cup plus 2 tbsp (270 ml) water

1¼ cups (280 g) sugar

1½ tsp (7 ml) freshly squeezed lemon juice

Separate the phyllo pastry sheets and lay them out on the countertop for a few hours to dry out completely; they should be bone dry and flaky. The time this will take depends on the temperature and humidity, so it will vary. You could leave them overnight to be sure. Arrange the sheets in a way that ensures they are fully exposed, otherwise some parts may retain moisture and take longer to dry.

Prepare a sling for the slow cooker according to the instructions on page 11.

Scrunch up the dried phyllo with your hands over a large bowl so it breaks into very small pieces. The pieces should be between a quarter and half a fingernail in size. Some pieces might be a bit smaller, which is okay.

In a separate bowl, whisk the olive oil, sunflower oil and sugar until smooth. Whisk in the eggs, then the baking powder, vanilla and orange zest. Using a spatula, fold the mixture into the phyllo pieces, ensuring they are all moistened, then transfer to the slow cooker insert. Even out the surface and cook on low for 2 hours if your slow cooker has an aluminum pot, or for 3 to 3½ hours if it has a ceramic pot.

As soon as the pie starts cooking, prepare the syrup so it can cool before it's used. Bring the orange zest, water and sugar to a boil in a small saucepan, turn the heat to medium and let the syrup bubble for 10 minutes. Remove from the heat, add the lemon juice and set aside to cool completely.

The pie is ready when the surface of the pie is set and has started to look crispy. Turn the slow cooker off. While it's still in the insert, slowly spoon the cooled syrup all over the hot pie so it's evenly absorbed. Let it sit until completely cool and remove it from the pot by lifting it with the foil "handles." Cut the pie into squares and serve.

Tip: I recommend using very fresh organic oranges for the best quality zest, with rich essential oils.

Note: If you have a 1-pound (454-g) package of phyllo pastry sheets (also known as fillo, or filo), be sure to use three-quarters of the total sheets provided. Due to the delicate nature of these thin sheets of dough, it is important to use the exact amount specified.

9-Ingredient Olive Oil Cake for St. Fanouris

(FANOUROPITA)

SERVES 8—10

Fanouropita isn't just another olive oil cake. Although its delicious taste and texture are enough to make it a great cake, it's also surrounded by religious tradition, which gives it an air of mystery and charm. Named after St. Fanouris, it's supposed to be made on the day the saint is celebrated, the 27th of August, and then offered to others.

The name comes from the verb *feno*, which means to reveal, and so it is said that making Fanouropita will result in good things being revealed to you. A job, something you lost, even a husband, if you're looking for one. Don't you just love how politically incorrect tradition can be!

The cake should always be made with an odd number of ingredients, ideally 7 or 9, as these are symbolic in Greek Orthodox faith. Mine has 9 if you don't count the powdered sugar, so I'm calling that optional to be on the safe side.

Regardless of religious tradition, this cake is delicious and ideal as an accompaniment to a hot cup of coffee or tea.

---

7 tbsp (105 ml) olive oil

¾ cup (180 ml) freshly squeezed orange juice

⅔ cup (140 g) sugar

2 cups (280 g) all-purpose flour, lightly packed

1 tsp baking powder

1 tsp cinnamon

¼ tsp baking soda

½ cup (85 g) sultanas, tightly packed

½ cup (60 g) coarsely chopped walnuts

Powdered sugar to decorate, optional

Create a sling for the slow cooker following the directions on page 11.

Beat the olive oil, orange juice and sugar together in a large mixing bowl until incorporated.

In a separate bowl, whisk the flour with the baking powder, cinnamon and baking soda, and beat it into the olive oil mixture.

Fold the sultanas and walnuts into the batter gently, until only just incorporated.

Pour the batter into the slow cooker and cover with a long piece of paper towel. The paper should sit tautly under the lid and not touch the batter. Cook on high for 1½ to 2 hours, or until the surface is set and a toothpick or cake tester comes out clean from the center of the cake.

Let it cool for a few minutes before turning out to cool completely (pull up the sling "handles" to do this easily). Dust with the sugar if using, cut into squares and serve.

Quince "Spoon Sweet" with Almonds

(GLYKO KYDONI)

YIELDS 4 CUPS (944 G)

Greek "spoon sweets," or *Glyka Koutaliou*, are fruit, or in some cases vegetables, boiled and preserved in a syrup of sugar and water. As the name suggests, the correct amount to serve is one heaped teaspoonful. To be honest, you probably couldn't eat more if you tried. They are devilishly sweet! Spoon sweets are some of the most traditional sweets of Greece and emerged from the need to preserve produce for use during the whole year.

Offering a homemade spoon sweet was once considered the ultimate way to welcome guests into one's home. It would be served in large bowls with lots of little spoons on the side for each guest to take their own, or individually on very small, pretty plates. With it, there would always be a refreshing glass of cold water.

This recipe is for one of the most common and well-loved spoon sweets ever: quince (*kydoni*). Quince cooks into a gorgeously vibrant pink sweet and is delicious on its own, the traditional way, or served over creamy, thick Greek yogurt. It's also a perfect accompaniment to a fresh white Greek cheese like manouri or anthotyro, which is similar to ricotta.

---

2 lb (900 g) quince, cut into very thin, matchstick-width strips

1 cup (140 g) whole blanched almonds

2²⁄₃ cups (600 g) sugar

Combine the quince and almonds in the slow cooker insert. Pour the sugar evenly over the top.

Cook on high for 7 to 8 hours, or until the quince is soft and the liquid is a runny syrup.

Store in jars in the refrigerator. The quince will last a couple of months.

Note: The result should not be thick or jam-like in consistency. The fruit should be soft but the syrup should stay fairly runny.

Coconut and Semolina Syrup Cake
(RAVANI)

A personal favorite, *Ravani* is a dessert originating from the Middle East, where it's known as *Basbousa*. Veria, in the North, is said to be the town with the absolute best Ravani—or Revani, as it's called there—in Greece. Legend has it that in 1886 a Turk gave a secret recipe to the owner of a local dairy shop that sold yogurt and sweets.

The authentic recipe calls for semolina and sheep's yogurt and doesn't include coconut; that came later. I'm happy it did; for me, it makes this cake extra delicious. Nowadays, variations are plentiful, but I think I can safely say this is the first slow cooker version.

For the cake

1 cup (225 g) sugar, divided

½ cup plus 2 tbsp (140 g) butter

3 eggs, separated

1½ cups (140 g) unsweetened desiccated coconut, plus extra for decorating

⅔ cup (85 g) all-purpose flour, lightly packed

½ cup (85 g) coarse semolina, lightly packed

1½ tsp (7 g) baking powder

¼ tsp salt

½ cup (120 ml) whole milk, divided

For the syrup

1 cup (240 ml) water

1 cup (225 g) sugar

1 (1 x 1-inch [2.5 x 2.5-cm]) piece of lemon peel

Reserve and set aside 1 tablespoon (12 g) of the sugar. Beat the rest of the sugar with the butter until fluffy, for about 10 minutes, using an electric mixer.

Prepare the slow cooker insert by making a sling, following the instructions on page 11.

Add the egg yolks to the butter and sugar mixture, and beat for about 5 minutes, until the color turns a pale yellow. Mix the coconut, flour, semolina, baking powder and salt in a separate bowl, using a whisk to get rid of any lumps. Add one-third of the coconut mixture to the egg mixture and beat until incorporated. Beat in half the milk. Repeat with the same quantities and then add the remaining coconut mixture at the end. Beat until smooth and set aside.

In a very clean bowl, beat the egg whites with the reserved tablespoon (12 g) of sugar until stiff peaks form, for about 6 to 7 minutes, using an electric whisk or a clean and dry mixer. Gently fold half the resulting meringue into the batter, then repeat with the other half until incorporated (no egg white should be visible).

Pour the batter into the lined slow cooker insert. Lay a long piece of paper towel over the top of the slow cooker and place the lid on to secure. The paper should not touch the batter; it should be lying just under the lid to catch condensation.

Cook on high for 1½ to 2 hours, or until the cake is set on top and a toothpick comes out clean or with a few dry crumbs when inserted into its center.

As soon as you turn on the slow cooker, make the syrup so it has time to cool. Bring the water, sugar and piece of lemon peel to a boil in a small saucepan. Turn the heat to medium and boil for 5 minutes. Set aside to cool completely.

When the cake is ready, turn the cooker off, remove the lid and immediately spoon the cooled syrup slowly over the top of the hot cake. Make sure to cover the whole surface, working slowly so that the cake has time to absorb the liquid.

Leave the Ravani in the slow cooker for a couple of hours to cool completely and soak up the syrup. Lift it out using the sling "handles" and sprinkle it with extra coconut flakes. Slice into diamond-shaped pieces and serve.

Easy, Milky, Greek Rice Pudding

SERVES 6

(RYZOGALO)

This recipe was my nemesis. Out of the whole book, it's the one with the most test-runs. My very first try was delicious and I thought I had it nailed. My mum, acting as recipe tester, found it great too. Then my other tester Constantina tried it. Oh, dear! The news was bad. I couldn't understand what the issue was. After hours of analyzing and agonizing, and after coming close to just rejecting the recipe from the list, we figured it out. My first version was thick and very rich, just the way Mum—who I remind you is English—likes it. This was the rice pudding of my childhood, or something very close to it. Constantina, on the other hand, was expecting something like the Greek version. I suddenly realized that yes, the Greek version is also delicious, but different. It's not as heavy, not as rich and not as wintry. In fact, it's a favorite dessert for summer, eaten cold from the fridge. And when you want to eat rice pudding cold, this is definitely the best way to make it. So here it is, my Greek rice pudding, best enjoyed on a hot afternoon with a sprinkle of cinnamon.

⅔ cup (140 g) arborio rice

⅔ cup (140 g) sugar

4 cups (960 ml) fresh whole milk

¼ tsp freshly grated orange zest, tightly packed

⅛ tsp salt

Powdered cinnamon, to serve

Combine the rice, sugar, milk, orange zest and salt in the slow cooker. Stir well and cook on low for 2 to 3 hours, or until the rice is soft and the milk has started to thicken. Stir well a couple of times during cooking.

The rice pudding will seem very runny with lots of creamy milk in the pot. As long as the rice is cooked and soft, the cooker should be turned off at this point. Continue to stir for a couple of minutes and then divide it into individual ramekins or little bowls. Chill in the refrigerator. The pudding will thicken when cold, but it's not supposed to set.

Serve with a generous sprinkling of cinnamon.

New Year's Eve Almond and Orange Cake

(VASILOPITA)

SERVES 8—10

It may be true that Easter is the most important holiday for Greek people, but Christmas and New Year are celebrated in equally good spirits, with equally good food. For the winter holidays, it's the sweets that take center stage, with *vasilopita* being the star of the show. Vasilopita is either a cake or a sweet bread—apart from a few rural areas in which it is a savory pie. It's made on New Year's Eve with a coin hidden inside and at the stroke of midnight, after exchanging good wishes, everyone gathers around to cut it. If your slice has the coin, you are in for a lucky year!

For cake-style vasilopita, delicious almond and orange combinations like this one are very popular. The fragrance, texture and flavor are quite special, with the glaze giving that extra sweetness and pleasant tang. Give it a different name, leave out the coin and you have my permission to make this cake any time of the year!

For the cake

1¼ cups (170 g) all-purpose flour, lightly packed

¾ cup (85 g) blanched almond meal, lightly packed

1 tsp baking powder

1 tsp powdered ginger

1 tsp powdered cardamom

¼ tsp salt

½ cup (110 g) butter, softened

1 cup (225 g) sugar

3 eggs

2 tbsp (30 g) orange zest

7 tbsp (105 ml) freshly squeezed orange juice

For the glaze

2 cups (200 g) powdered sugar, lightly packed

3-4 tbsp (45-60 ml) freshly squeezed orange juice

Make a sling for the slow cooker insert following the instructions on page 11.

Whisk the flour, almond meal, baking powder, ginger, cardamom and salt in a bowl.

In a separate bowl or the bowl of a stand mixer, beat the butter and sugar until light and fluffy, for about 10 minutes. Slowly add each egg to the butter mixture, beating well between additions. Then add the orange zest and beat to incorporate.

Next, beat one-third of the flour mixture into the egg mixture, followed by half the orange juice and repeat, beating in between each addition. Add the remaining flour mixture and beat only until incorporated and no flour is visible. Don't overmix at this stage.

Transfer the cake batter to the slow cooker. Lay a piece of paper towel over the top of the insert, and put the lid on to secure it in place. The paper towel should not be touching the batter, but just sitting under the glass lid to absorb condensation.

Cook on high for 1½ to 2 hours, or until the top is set and a knife or toothpick inserted in the center of the cake comes out clean or with some dry crumbs. Let the cake cool for a few minutes and turn it out using the sling "handles."

To make the glaze, whisk the powdered sugar with 2 tablespoons (30 ml) of orange juice. Whisk well, even if at first it looks like it needs more liquid. If it is still too dry, add a few more drops of juice and whisk again. Do this until the glaze reaches the desired consistency. It should be runny enough for you to pour, but very slow-moving when you do.

After the cake has cooled completely, pour the glaze over the top and let it set.

If you are making vasilopita for New Year's Eve, you can follow the Greek tradition of the lucky coin. When the cake is cooked and before you glaze it, cover a small coin with aluminum foil and press it into the bottom of the cake in a random spot, but not the center. Don't press it so far in that it shows on top. Continue with the glazing and try to forget where you put the coin! When cutting the cake, say the name of the person who will get each slice before you actually cut it.

ACKNOWLEDGMENTS

Wow! Here I am, writing my thank yous. I can't quite believe it. It's been a hell of a rollercoaster and I'm so glad that the following people were with me on this crazy ride.

First and foremost, my supercool publisher, for discovering me in my little corner of the Internet and believing in my idea.

My editor, Marissa, and the rest of the gang over at Page Street, who patiently answered a gazillion questions, explained everything in way more detail than they had to and helped make this book happen.

My blog readers for being there, even though writing this book took me away from them for a while.

My friend Constantina for . . . gosh, where do I even start? Project manager, taste tester, recipe tester, recipe proofreader, photo and styling assistant and holder of the whip that got me into shape. Constantina, thank you, for the hours and hours of your life that you devoted to me and my project. For celebrating with me when I was excited, for encouraging me when I was doubting myself and for ignoring me when I was being obnoxious. It was just the stress, you know that!

My mum, Deborah, who has been ignoring such stress-induced obnoxious outbursts my whole life. Apart from putting up with me, her role suddenly included that of taste tester, recipe tester, extensive proofreader and receiver of lengthy telephone calls to discuss—in agonizing detail—the types of celery one might find in the US. Mum, I can't thank you enough.

My auntie Anna, who spent the first ten days of her holiday in Greece tirelessly proofreading my manuscript with painstaking attention to detail, while getting up at ungodly hours to meet the deadline and sometimes even forgetting to eat. Anna, thank you so much, and I promise to stop putting commas before the word "and." Or to at least try!

My neighbors Oliver, Nancy and Philippos, who tasted every single dish that's in here and never balked at the sight of yet another mountain of food coming their way. Guys, thanks for answering the door every time.

And of course, my partner George, a.k.a the Mister, for everything. For supporting me emotionally and practically, for hearing me go on and on about my failures and successes, for urging me to move forward when I didn't think I could. George, thank you for not wondering (at least out loud) why we were eating take-out, yet again, when I'd just spent the whole day, week, month . . . cooking.

ABOUT THE AUTHOR

ELENI VONISSAKOU is a full-time food blogger and self-taught recipe developer, food stylist and photographer. She is half English and half Greek and lives just outside Athens, Greece, with her partner George and their boisterous golden retriever, Westley. Her bilingual food blog, The Foodie Corner, was born in 2013. Since then, she has cooked on national TV several times and her recipes have been featured on websites such as The Huffington Post, Buzzfeed, Greatist and Greek print and digital publications including *Elle*, *Shape*, the Sunday pull-out *Real Taste* and *WWF*. Slow cookers are especially close to her heart, with a dedicated category on the blog and a business importing and selling them in Greece. You can find her at thefoodiecorner.net or follow her on Facebook (facebook.com/thefoodiecorner.gr) and Instagram (@thefoodiecorner).

INDEX